INVESTING FOR BEGINNERS

A Step By Step Guide to Start Investing – Stock Market, Forex Trading, Futures, ETFs and Cryptocurrency

Carl Hitoshi

TABLE OF CONTENTS

Introduction

The "Investing for beginners: A Step By Step Guide to Start Investing" offers a simplified but complete introduction to the world of investing.

Here you can find a lot of ideas for start investing, and many theoretical concepts to start learning about professional Investments.

We will talk about some side of investment, like Stock Market, Forex trading, Future, ETFs and Cryptocurrency.

All of them will can help you to create passive income and starting to create economic capital who you will use for bigger investment.

What can you learn?

-A step-by-step instruction on how to make your first trade

-What the stock market is and why it is a big opportunity if you know what to do

-Introduction to Forex

-Introduction to futures trading

-Differences between technical analysis and fundamental analysis

- How investors with small capitals can be helped by leverage

-Why it's important to diversify a portfolio and how do it

-How to set right mindset against any losses

-A simplified dictionary with the most important terms

This book is perfect for anyone who wants to start investing and don't know how to do, and Experience investor who want to master investments with relative strategies too.

STOCK MARKETS

History of the Stock Market

Over two hundred years ago private banks began to sell stock to raise money to expand. This was a new way to invest and a way for the rich to get richer. In 1792 twenty-four large merchants agreed to form a market known as the New York Stock Exchange (NYSE). They agreed to meet daily on Wall Street and buy and sell stocks.

By the mid-1800s the United States was experiencing rapid growth. Companies began to sell stock to raise money for the expansion necessary to meet the growing demand for their products and services. The people who bought this stock became part owners of the company and shared in the profits or loss of the company.

A new form of investing began to emerge when investors realized that they could sell their stock to others. This is where speculation began to influence an investor's decision to buy or sell and led the way to large fluctuations in stock prices.

Originally investing in the stock market was confined to the very wealthy. Now stock ownership has found its way to all sectors of our society.

What is a Stock?

A stock certificate is a piece of paper declaring that you own a piece of the company. Companies sell stock to finance expansion, hire people, advertise, etc. In general, the sale of stock help companies grows. The people who buy the stock share in the profits or losses of the company.

Trading of stock is generally driven by short term speculation about the company operations, products, services, etc. It is this speculation that influences an investor's decision to buy or sell and what prices are attractive.

The company raises money through the primary market. This is the Initial Public Offering (IPO). Thereafter, the stock is traded in the secondary market (what we call the stock market) when individual investors or traders buy and sell the shares to each other. The company is not involved in any profit or loss from this secondary market.

Technology and the Internet have made the stock market available to the mainstream public. Computers have made investing in the stock market very easy. Market and company news are available almost anywhere in the world. The Internet has brought a vast new group of investors into the stock market and this group continues to grow each year.

Investing in the stock markets

Over the past few years, the stock market has made substantial declines. Some short-term investors have lost a good bit of money. Many new stock market investors look at this and become very skeptical about getting in now.

If you are considering investing in the stock market, it is very important that you understand how the markets work. All of the financial and market data that the newcomer is bombarded with can leave them confused and overwhelmed.

The stock market is an everyday term used to describe a place where stock in companies is bought and sold. Companies issues stock to finance new equipment, buy other companies, expand their business, introduce new products and services, etc. The investors who buy this stock now own a share of the company. If the company does well the price of their stock increases. If the company does not do well the stock price decreases. If the price that you sell your stock for is more than you paid for it, you have made money.

When you buy stock in a company you share in the profits and losses of the company until you sell your stock or the company goes out of business. Studies have shown that long term stock ownership has been one of the best investment strategies for most people.

People buy stocks on a tip from a friend, a phone call from a broker, or a recommendation from a TV analyst. They buy during a strong market. When the market later begins to decline, they panic and sell for a loss. This is the typical horror story we hear from people who have no investment strategy.

Before committing your hard-earned money to the stock market, it will behoove you to consider the risks and benefits of doing so. You must have an investment strategy. This strategy will define what and when to buy and when you will sell it.

Bull Market - Bear Market

Anyone who has been following the stock market or watching TV news is probably familiar with the terms Bull Market and Bear Market. What do they mean?

A bull market is defined by steadily rising prices. The economy is thriving and companies are generally making a profit. Most investors feel that this trend will continue for some time. By contrast a bear market is one where prices are dropping. The economy is probably in a decline and many companies are experiencing difficulties. Now the investors are pessimistic about the future profitability of the stock market. Since investors' attitudes tend to drive their willingness to buy or sell these trends normally perpetuate themselves until significant outside events intervene to cause a reversal of opinion.

In a bull market the investor hopes to buy early and hold the stock until it has reached it's high. Obviously, predicting the low and high is impossible. Since most investors are "bullish" they make more money in the rising bull market. They are willing to invest more money as the stock is rising and realize more profit.

Investing in a bear market incurs the greatest possibility of losses because the trend is downward and there is no end in sight. An investment strategy in this case might be short selling. Short selling is selling a stock that you don't own. You can make arrangements with your broker to do this. You will in effect be borrowing shares from your broker to sell in the hope of buying them back later when the price has dropped. You will profit from the difference in the two prices. Another strategy for a bear market would be buying defensive stocks. These are stocks like utility companies that are not affected by the market downturn or companies that sell their products during all economic conditions.

Brokers

Traditionally, investors bought and sold stock through large brokerage houses. They made a phone call to their broker who relayed their order to the exchange floor. These brokers also offered their services as stock advisors to people who knew very little about the market. These people relied on their broker to guide them and paid a hefty price in commissions and fees as a result. The advent of the Internet has led to a new class of brokerage houses. These firms provide on-line accounts where you may log in and buy and sell stocks from anywhere you can get an Internet connection. They usually don't offer any market advice and only provide order execution. The Internet investor can find some good deals as the members of this new breed of electronic brokerage houses compete for your business!

Blue Chip Stocks

Large well-established firms who have demonstrated good profitability and growth, dividend payout, and quality products and services are called blue chip stocks. They are usually the leaders of their industry, have been around for a long time, and are considered to be among the safest investments. Blue chip stocks are included in the Dow Jones Industrial Average, an index composed of thirty companies who are leaders in their industry groups. They are very popular among individual and institutional investors. Blue chip stocks attract investors who are interested in consistent dividends and growth as well as stability. They are rarely subject to the price volatility of other stocks and their share prices will normally be higher than other categories of stock. The downside of blue chips is that due to their stability they won't appreciate as rapidly as compared to smaller up-and-coming stocks.

Penny Stocks

Penny Stocks are very low-priced stocks and are very risky. They are usually issued by companies without a long-term record of stability or profitability.

The appeal of penny stock is their low price. Though the odds are against it, if the company can get into a growth trend the share price can jump very rapidly. They are usually favored by the speculative investor.

Income Stocks

Income Stocks are stock that normally pay higher than average dividends. They are well established companies like utilities or telephone companies. Income stocks are popular with the investor who wants to own the stock for a long time and collect the dividends and who is not so interested in a gain in share price.

Value Stocks

Sometimes a company's earnings and growth potential indicate that its share price should be higher than it is currently trading at. These stocks are said to be Value Stocks.

For the most part, the market and investors have ignored them. The investor who buys a value stock hopes that the market will soon realize what a bargain it is and begin to buy. This would drive up the share price.

Defensive Stocks

Defensive Stocks are issued by companies in industries that have demonstrated good performance in bad markets. Food and utility companies are defensive stocks.

Market Timing

One of the most well-known market quotes is: "Buy Low - Sell High". To be consistently successful in the stock market one needs strategy, discipline, knowledge, and tools. We need to understand our strategy and stick with it. This will prevent us from being distracted by emotion, panic, or greed.

One of the most prominent investing strategies used by "investment pros" is Market Timing. This is the attempt to predict future prices from past market performance. Forecasting stock prices has been a problem for as long as people have been trading stocks. The time to buy or sell a stock is based on a number of economic indicators derived from company analysis, stock charts, and various complex mathematical and computer-based algorithms.

RISKS

There are numerous risks involved in investing in the stock market. Knowing that these risks exist should be one of the things an investor is constantly aware of. The money you invest in the stock market is not guaranteed. For instance, you might buy a stock expecting a certain dividend or rate of share price increase. If the company experiences financial problems it may not live up to your dividend or price growth expectations. If the company goes out of business you will probably lose everything you invested in it. Due to the uncertainty of the outcome, you bear a certain amount of risk when you purchase a stock.

Stocks differ in the amount of risks they present. For instance, Internet stocks have demonstrated themselves to be much riskier than utility stocks.

One risk is the stocks reaction to news items about the company. Depending on how the investors interpret the new item, they may be influenced to buy or sell the stock. If enough of these investors begin to buy or sell at the same time it will cause the price to rise or fall.

One effective strategy to cope with risk is diversification. This means spreading out your investments over several stocks in different market sectors. Remember the saying: "Don't put all your eggs in the same basket".

As investors we need to find our "Risk Tolerance". Risk tolerance is our emotional and financial ability to ride out a decline in the market without panicking and selling at a loss.

When we define that point, we make sure not to extend our investments beyond it.

BENEFITS

The same forces that bring risk into investing in the stock market also make possible the large gains many investors enjoy. It's true that the fluctuations in the market make for losses as well as gains but if you have a proven strategy and stick with it over the long term you will be a winner!

The Internet has made investing in the stock market a possibility for almost everybody. The wealth of online information, articles, and stock quotes gives the average person the same abilities that were once available to only stock brokers. No longer does the investor need to contact a broker for this information or to place orders to buy or sell. We now have almost instant access to our accounts and the ability to place on-line orders in seconds. This new freedom has ushered in new masses of hopeful investors. Still this in not a random process of buying and selling stock. We need a strategy for selecting a suitable stock as well as timing to buy and sell in order to make a profit.

Day Trading

Day Trading is the attempt to buy and sell stock over a very short period of time. The day trader hopes to cash in on the short-term fluctuations in a stock's price. It would not be unusual for the day trader to buy and sell the same stock in a matter of a few minutes or to buy and sell the same stock several times a day.

Day traders sit in front of computer monitors all day looking for short term movement in a stock. They then attempt to get in on the movement before it reverses. The real day trader does not hold a stock overnight due to the risk of some event or news item triggering the stock to reverse direction. It takes intense concentration to monitor the minute by minute movement of several stocks.

Day trading involves a great deal of risk because of the uncertainty of the market behavior over the short term. The slightest economic or political news can cause a stock to fluctuate wildly and result in unexpected losses.

There are a few people who make respectable gains day trading. The people who probably make the most are the selfproclaimed "experts" who sell the books or operate the web sites that cater to the day trader. Because of the profits to be made from sales to people who want to get rich quick, they make it seem as attractive as possible. The truth is that in the long run more people lose than gain by day trading. This does not translate into a very good investment.

WAYS TO ENSURE SUCCESS IN TRADING STOCKS

Make it a habit to keep off your emotions from your investments

By far the largest obstacle quite a large number of beginners have to routinely face is their inability to regulate their emotions and proceed to make logical decisions. In the short term, the prices of company stocks correspond with the combined emotions of the whole investment community. When most stock market investors happen to be anxious about a particular firm, its stock prices will be bound to take a plunge. Alternatively, when most traders possess a positive perspective to a firm, its stock prices will naturally rise.

Those individuals who retain a negative perspective about the stock market are known as 'bears'. While those that have positive outlooks to the same are known as 'bulls.' During market hours, the unceasing struggle between bulls and bears is usually reflected on the constantly fluctuating securities' prices. These short-term fluctuations generally arise from rumors, speculations and in some cases even hope. All of these factors can be rightly labeled as been emotions. Effective stock market investment necessitates a logical and systematic analysis of a company's assets, management and future prospects.

At this juncture, it is important for you to remember that stock market prices can move in contrast to most expectations. For the inexperienced, this can fuel insecurity and tension. At such moments, you will find yourself faced with a dilemma - "Should you sell your position to prevent a loss?", "Or should you continue maintaining your position in the hope that the prices will ultimately rebound?" Even in the occasions that prices perform as you expected, you will still find yourself facing troubling questions. "Should you take a profit now prior to the prices falling?", "Or should you maintain your position as the prices could rise even higher?"

Dealing with all these perplexing thoughts can trigger a lot of worry, particularly if you constantly monitor the prices of the securities you trade in. This emotion can eventually prompt you take certain actions. As your emotions are the main motivation, it is mostly likely your action will be wrong. When you buy a stock, you should only do so for valid reasons. Also, you should have realistic expectations of exactly how the prices will perform if your guiding reasons prove to be accurate. Finally, before investing in any stock, always take time to determine the exact point you will liquidate your holdings, especially if your reasons are proven wrong. All in all, always have an appropriate 'exit' strategy prior to purchasing any stock, and make it a point to execute it unemotionally.

Make it your business to comprehensively learn about the basics of stock market investment.

Prior to making your very first stock market investment or trade, make sure that you fully understand all the basics of stock market together with the individual securities which make them up. Below are some of the most pertinent areas you will be obliged to be well conversant with before commencing any stock market activities.

To begin with, take time to understand the exact financial metrics as well as definition that are utilized in stock market trading. Some of the most notable of which are P/E ratio, earnings / share, return on equity and compound annual growth rate. Take you time to fully grasp how these metrics are usually calculated. It is important to state that been in a position of effectively contrasting just how companies use these metrics is essential in any successful stock market investment operations.

Next you should learn all about the most popular techniques of stock selection and timing. To this end, you should make it a point to understand how fundamental and technical analysis can be executed. More importantly, just how they vary and when it is appropriate to use them in a stock market trading strategy. You should also be well conversant with the different types of stock market orders. Take all the time you require to fully comprehend just how market orders, limit orders, stop market orders, stop limit orders and trailing stop loss orders vary from each other.

Finally, you should make it a point to learn all you can on the different kinds of stock market investment accounts which are made available. You perhaps are well conversant with cash accounts that are arguably the most prevalently used by stock market investors. Nevertheless, what are known as margin accounts are by regulations, required when you wish to make some specific types of stock market trades. So, make sure you fully understand how margin accounts can be calculated. You should also find out about the exact differences between initial and maintenance margin accounts prerequisites.

Make it a point to diversify your stock market investments

The moment you have performed all the necessary research that helps you determine and even quantify risk, making the decision to diversify your stock market portfolio can be a very shrewd step. The same is also the case, when you are totally 'comfortable' that you will be able to pinpoint any potential danger which might jeopardize your position in a stress-free manner. In both scenarios, you will be able to liquidate your stock market investments prior to sustaining any dangerous loss.

Therefore, the most prudent means of been able to effectually manage stock market investment risks is to diversify your exposure. You should know that most shrewd stock market investors, make it their business to own stocks from different firms, different sectors and even different nations. The primary driving force which motivates them to do so is the firm guarantee that a single inauspicious event can never influence all their holdings. What all this really boils down to is the undeniable fact that stock diversification can allow to comfortably recover from the loss of a single and even several of your investments.

INVESTING IN CRYPTOCURRENCY

Cryptocurrency is the newest trend in the money market that contains the elements of computer science and mathematical theory. Its primary function is to secure communication as it converts legible information into an unbreakable code. You can track your purchases and transfers with cryptocurrency. Following are the top ten tips for investors to invest in cryptocurrency.

It's Just Like Investing in Commodities:

Investing in cryptocurrency is just like investing in any other commodity. It has two faces - it can be used as an asset or as an investment, which you can sell and exchange.

Buy Bitcoin Directly:

Buy Bitcoins directly if you do not want to pay the fee for investing or if you are interested in possessing real Bitcoins. There are a lot of options all over the world including Bitcoin.de, BitFinex, and BitFlyer from where you can buy Bitcoins directly.

Only an Absolute Minority Uses Cryptocurrency:

Today, Bitcoin is the most common cryptocurrency in the world of investment. In the United States, only 24% of the adults know about it, and surprisingly only 2% Americans use it. It is good news for the financial investors as the low usage represents a fruitful investment for the future.

Usage is Growing:

The combined market cap of the cryptocurrencies is more than 278 billion American dollars. It includes all cryptocurrencies in existence including hundreds of smaller and unknown ones. The real-time usage of the cryptocurrencies has gone up, showing a rise in trend.

Usage is the Key Criteria:

As an investor, the usage must be the key for you. The demand and supply data of cryptocurrencies exhibits a decent investment opportunity right now. There exists a strong usage of the currencies for facilitating payments between financial institutions and thus, pushing transaction costs down meaningfully.

It will Solve Problems for You:

Money is to solve problems, and so is the cryptocurrency. The bigger problem it solves, the higher potential value it gets. The sweet spot for possessing cryptocurrency is that it provides access to money and basic bank functions including paying and wiring.

Crypto to Money:

Today, cryptocurrencies can be exchanged to conventional paper money. Therefore, the lock-in risk that existed a while ago is gone now.

Create Your Portfolio:

Since cryptocurrencies are exchangeable, they have become another way to build your portfolio. You can now store cash in the form of crypto and exchange it for cash anytime you need the traditional money.

Read the Right Resources

What cryptocurrencies are available and how do I buy them?

With a market cap of about $278 billion, Bitcoin is the most established cryptocurrency. Ethereum is second with a market cap of over $74 billion. Besides these two currencies, there are a number of other options as well, including Ripple ($28B), Litecoin ($17B), and MIOTA ($13B).

Being first to market, there are a lot of exchanges for Bitcoin trade all over the world. BitStamp and Coinbase are two wellknown US-based exchanges. Bitcoin.de is an established European exchange. If you are interested in trading other digital currencies along with Bitcoin, then a crypto marketplace is where you will find all the digital currencies in one place.

What options do I have to store my money?

Another important consideration is storage of the coins. One option, of course, is to store it on the exchange where you buy them. However, you will have to be careful in selecting the exchange. The popularity of digital currencies has resulted in many new, unknown exchanges popping up everywhere. Take the time to do your due diligence so you can avoid the scammers.

Another option you have with cryptocurrencies is that you can store them yourself. One of the safest options for storing your investment is hardware wallets. Companies like Ledger allow you store Bitcoins and several other digital currencies as well.

What's the market like and how can I learn more about it?

The cryptocurrency market fluctuates a lot. The volatile nature of the market makes it more suited for a long-term play.

There are many established news sites that report on digital currencies, including Coindesk, Business Insider, Coin Telegraph, and Cryptocoin News. Besides these sites, there are also many Twitter accounts that tweet about digital currencies, including BitcoinRTs and AltCoinCalendar.

Digital currencies aim to disrupt the traditional currency and commodity market. While these currencies still have a long way to go, the success of Bitcoins and Ethereum have proven that there is genuine interest in the concept. Understanding the basics of cryptocurrency investment will help you start in the right way.

FOREX TRADING

Introduction

Chances are, you were attracted to Forex trading because you want to earn an extra income and perhaps even gain freedom from a job that you hate. I'm sure that you found out pretty quickly that trading Forex profitably is no walk in the park! Beginner Forex traders face many challenges in their pursuit of Forex trading profits, and it's a sad fact that 90% of them don't survive past their first year of trading.

Many new Forex traders are lured into the world of Forex by the promise of easy riches, but the truth is that trading Forex is a risky business. If you don't know what you're doing when you're just getting started in Forex, you can easily lose all of your investment capital, and even end up owing large sums of money! Clearly, there are many hidden pitfalls in learning to trade Forex that you need to be aware of, so that you can avoid them on your way to success in Forex.

Forex Trading: A Beginner's Guide

The forex market is the world's largest international currency trading market operating non-stop during the working week. Most forex trading is done by professionals such as bankers. Generally, forex trading is done through a forex broker - but there is nothing to stop anyone trading currencies. Forex currency trading allows buyers and sellers to buy the currency they need for their business and sellers who have earned currency to exchange what they have for a more convenient currency. The world's largest banks dominate forex and according to a survey in The Wall Street Journal Europe, the ten most active traders who are engaged in forex trading account for almost 73% of trading volume.

However, a sizeable proportion of the remainder of forex trading is speculative with traders building up an investment which they wish to liquidate at some stage for profit. While a currency may increase or decrease in value relative to a wide range of currencies, all forex trading transactions are based upon currency pairs. So, although the Euro may be 'strong' against a basket of currencies, traders will be trading in just one currency pair and may simply concern themselves with the Euro/US Dollar (EUR/USD) ratio. Changes in relative values of currencies may be gradual or triggered by specific events such as are unfolding at the time of writing this - the toxic debt crisis.

Because the markets for currencies are global, the volumes traded every day are vast. For the large corporate investors, the great benefits of trading on Forex are:

- Enormous liquidity - over \$4 trillion per day, that's \$4,000,000,000. This means that there's always someone ready to trade with you

- Every one of the world's free currencies are traded - this means that you may trade the currency you want at any time

- Twenty-four - hour trading during the 5-day working week

- Operations are global which mean that you can trade with any part of the world at any time

From the point of view of the smaller trader there's lots of benefits too, such as:

- A rapidly-changing market - that's one which is always changing and offering the chance to make money

- Very well-developed mechanisms for controlling risk

- Ability to go long or short - this means that you can make money either in rising or falling markets

- Leverage trading - meaning that you can benefit from large volume trading while having a relatively-low capital base

- Lots of options for zero-commission trading

How the forex Market Works

As forex is all about foreign exchange, all transactions are made up from a currency pair - say, for instance, the Euro and the US Dollar. The basic tool for trading forex is the exchange rate which is expressed as a ratio between the values of the two currencies such as EUR/USD = 1.4086. This value, which is referred to as the 'forex rate' means that, at that particular time, one Euro would be worth 1.4086 US Dollars. This ratio is always expressed to 4 decimal places which means that you could see a forex rate of EUR/USD = 1.4086 or EUR/USD = 1.4087 but never EUR/USD = 1.40865. The rightmost digit of this ratio is referred to as a 'pip'. So, a change from EUR/USD = 1.4086 to EUR/USD = 1.4088 would be referred to as a change of 2 pips. One pip, therefore is the smallest unit of trade.

With the forex rate at EUR/USD = 1.4086, an investor purchasing 1000 Euros using dollars would pay $1,408.60. If the forex rate then changed to EUR/USD = 1.5020, the investor could sell their 1000 Euros for $1,502.00 and bank the $93.40 as profit. If this doesn't seem to be large amount to you, you have to put the sum into context. With a rising or falling market, the forex rate does not simply change in a uniform way but oscillates and profits can be taken many times per day as a rate oscillates around a trend.

When you're expecting the value EUR/USD to fall, you might trade the other way by selling Euros for dollars and buying then back when the forex rate has changed to your advantage.

Is forex Risky?

When you trade on forex as in any form of currency trading, you're in the business of currency speculation and it is just that - speculation. This means that there is some risk involved in forex currency trading as in any business but you might and should, take steps to minimize this. You can always set a limit to the downside of any trade, that means to define the maximum loss that you are prepared to accept if the market goes against you - and it will on occasions.

The best insurance against losing your shirt on the forex market is to set out to understand what you're doing totally. Search the internet for a good forex trading tutorial and study it in detail- a bit of good forex education can go a long way. When there's bits you don't understand, look for a good forex trading forum and ask lots and lots of questions. Many of the people who habitually answer your queries on this will have a good forex trading blog and this will probably not only give you answers to your questions but also provide lots of links to good sites. Be vigilant, however, watch out for forex trading scams.

Don't be too quick to part with your money and investigate anything very well before you shell out any hard-earned money!

The Forex Trading Systems

While you may be right in being cautious about any forex trading system that's advertised, there are some good ones around. Most of them either utilize forex charts and by means of these, identify forex trading signals which tell the trader when to buy or sell. These signals will be made up of a particular change in a forex rate or a trend and these will have been devised by a forex trader who has studied long-term trends in the market so as to identify valid signals when they occur. Many of the systems will use forex trading software which identifies such signals from data inputs which are gathered automatically from market information sources. Some utilize automated forex trading software which can trigger trades automatically when the signals tell it to do so. If these sounds too good to be true to you, look around for online forex trading systems which will allow you undertake some dummy trading to test them out. By doing this, you can get some forex trading training by giving them a spin before you put real money on the table.

How Much do you Need to Start off with?

This is a bit of a 'How long is a piece of string?' question but there are ways for to be beginner to dip a toe into the water without needing a fortune to start with. The minimum trading size for most trades on forex is usually 100,000 units of any currency and this volume is referred to as a standard "lot".

However, there are many firms which offer the facility to purchase in dramatically-smaller lots than this and a bit of internet searching will soon locate these. There's many adverts quoting only a couple of hundred dollars to get going

Where do You Start?

The single most obvious answer is of course - on the internet! Online forex trading gives you direct access to the forex market and there's lots and lots of companies out there who are in business just to deal with you online. Be vigilant, do spend the time to get some good forex trading education, again this can be provided online and set up your dummy account to trade before you attempt to go live. If you take care and take your time, there's no reason why you shouldn't be successful in forex trading so, have patience and stick at it!

THE PROBLEMS BEGINNER FOREX TRADERS FACE

The biggest problem you'll face as a beginner Forex trader is a lack of time. After all, you're probably working full time as it is, and have a family full of loved ones who are important to you. In between your job and your family/social time, there's not a lot left to learn how to trade Forex from scratch. It normally takes 2-3 years for anyone getting started in Forex to achieve a level of skill necessary to earn a consistent income through trading Forex, and that requires you to be committed to spending all of your after-work hours in front of your computer learning trading the hard way.

Even if you're willing to commit the time to learn how to trade Forex on your own, there's a chronic lack of quality, organized information on how to progress from where you are now to where you want to be. There's a whole lot of information out there, but as far as what works and what doesn't, you're very much on your own to figure that out. And even if you do figure it all out, and become one of the elite 5% group of profitable Forex traders, you'll just have a new job: Forex trading.

The Solution: Automatic Forex Trading Systems

If you don't see yourself going through this long, hard process and if you'd much rather have the Forex trading profits right now, then there's only one way that you can do it: automatic Forex trading systems. Maybe you're not aware of this, but there are professionally designed FX trading systems that can do the trading for you on complete autopilot. You simply buy them, link it up with your Metatrader 4 trading platform, and it will do all the buying and selling for you while you work, play and sleep. With automatic Forex trading systems, you get your Forex trading profits right now, you don't have to be chained to your computer after working hours, and you don't have to learn how to trade Forex on your own.

So, what's the catch? Surely automatic Forex trading systems are too good to be true, otherwise everyone would be getting rich with them already. Yes, there is a catch: most people don't know what good FX trading systems are. They think that FX trading systems that promise to double or triple their gains in a matter of days are good, and they look for systems that win 90+% of the time, but these are actually really bad systems that will wipe out your account one day.

The best automatic Forex trading systems are often understated: they tend to win closer to 60% of the time, and they "only" make returns of 5-10% a month. Well, that's nothing to turn your nose at, considering the state of the economy and other traditional investment vehicles, and with smart money management and the power of compounding, you can create a lasting Forex passive income that can give you the financial freedom you desire.

THE DOWNFALL OF SCALPING FOREX TRADE SYSTEMS

The truth is, trading is one of the most mundane and unexciting things to do if you're doing it right. Excitement and fun come from uncertainty: you take a trade and you hope that it will be a winner, but you don't really know where it's going. That's not trading, it's gambling. Real trading is run like a business, with automated processes in place to collect pips from the market, and you know roughly what to expect from your automatic Forex trading system in the long run.

That said, automatic Forex trading systems can't completely eliminate the need to feel the rush of trading Forex. Subconsciously, when you choose a system that trades very frequently and has a very high promised percentage of winners, you're indulging that need for a rush. After all, we all love to win and specially to win a lot. There's even a special kind of system called Scalping Forex Trading Systems that cater to the need for many winning trades.

Scalping Forex Trading Systems typically trade very frequently, often between 10-20 times a day and even more sometimes.

They aim to collect 5-10 pips in profit at a time, and are often in and out in less than an hour. This constant turnover creates a string of many profitable trades in a row, which is exactly what Forex traders like to see. The catch though, is that when it loses, and believe me it does lose, it will often lose 100 pips or more. That means that you could have 10 winners and just one loss, and you could still be net -10 pips for your account.

Why Trading Less Is More in Forex

Having an automatic Forex trading system that trades frequently also means that you pay more in spread to your Forex broker than if you used a less frequently trading system. The spread costs add up to thousands of dollars in the long run, so with a system that trades frequently you'll only be making huge profits for your Forex broker, and not yourself. An automatic Forex trading system that trades less is to your benefit because you're saving a significant amount of money in spread costs, and keeping more of the profits for yourself.

If you're looking for an automatic Forex trading system, then you're better off with ones that trade less frequently, and aim for more profits on each trade. Of course, your winning percentage will decrease, but your profit per trade will increase and your loss per trade will decrease. That means that you won't run the risk of blowing days of profits in one losing trade, and have a much more stable return on investment. So, if you want the best automatic trading results, then forget about Scalping Forex Trading Systems and get yourself a system that trades less, for more.

BEGINNER FOREX TRADING MISTAKES

It's a well-known fact that 95% of traders getting started in Forex don't make it past their first year of trading. The biggest mistake that beginner Forex traders make is that they believe that trading Forex is easy. They believe that they can double their money in a matter of weeks or even days, and as a result they get overaggressive in their trading. They open up many positions, often putting all their capital at risk. The result is that they may get mind boggling gains when the markets are in their favor, but lose it all and even blow up their account in a matter of hours when it all goes wrong.

The truth is, it's one of the most difficult skills to learn, because of the randomness that is in the Forex markets. You need to know that you can't make 100% gains in a few weeks, and you can't turn $1000 into a million dollars. When you understand that trading Forex is not an easy thing, especially when you're just getting started in Forex, then you're far ahead of the crowd in your journey to make a Forex trading income.

Succeeding Where Others Have Failed

To succeed in Forex where all the others have failed, you need to adjust your attitude to consider trading Forex a difficult thing to do. This core belief will help you to avoid the common beginner Forex trading mistakes, and aid you in learning to trade Forex profitably. When you realize that trading is difficult, you'll know that as a trader who's getting started in Forex, you need more than you have right now to achieve a Forex trading income.

Contrary to what anyone else will tell you, you don't need to spend years of your life learning to trade Forex. All you need is a profitable Forex trading system, and a cautious attitude towards money management in your trades. As someone who is getting started in Forex, you may not have the necessary knowledge and experience in the markets, but you can use the help of Forex traders who have already gone through the school of hard knocks so that you don't have to. There are a few profitable Forex trading systems that are developed by successful traders for beginner Forex traders that you can use to start making money from Forex right away.

The key advantage that you have is your cautious attitude towards Forex trading. While many traders fail even with profitable Forex trading systems because they think that trading Forex is easy, you will have the right mindset and the right methods combined to allow you to avoid all the Forex trading mistakes that kill their chances of success. From this point on, all you need to do is to stay consistent and collect your Forex trading income each and every month!

DIFFERENCE BETWEEN STOCK TRADING AND FOREX TRADING

The forex (foreign currency exchange) market is the largest and most liquid financial market in the world. The forex market unlike stock markets is an over-the-counter market with no central exchange and clearing house where orders are matched.

Traditionally forex trading has not been popular with retail traders/investors (traders takes shorter term positions than investors) because forex market was only opened to Hedge Funds and was not accessible to retail traders like us. Only in recent years that forex trading is opened to retail traders. Comparatively stock trading has been around for much longer for retail investors. Recent advancement in computer and trading technologies has enabled low commission and easy access to retail traders to trade stock or foreign currency exchange from almost anywhere in the world with internet access. Easy access and low commission have tremendously increased the odds of winning for retail traders, both in stocks and forex. Which of the two is a better option for a trader? The comparisons of retail stock trading and retail forex trading are as follows;

Nature of the Instrument

The nature of the items being bought and sold between forex trading and stocks trading are different. In stocks trading, a trader is buying or selling a share in a specific company in a country. There are many different stock markets in the world. Many factors determine the rise or fall of a stock price. Refer to my article in under stock section to find more information about the factors that affect stock prices. Forex trading involves buying or selling of currency pairs. In a transaction, a trader buys a currency from one country, and sells the currency from another country. Therefore, the term "exchange". The trader is hoping that the value of the currency that he buys will rise with respect to the value of the currency that he sells. In essence, a forex trader is betting on the economic prospect (or at least her monetary policy) of one country against another country.

Market Size & Liquidity

Forex market is the largest market in the world. With daily transactions of over US$4 trillion, it dwarfs the stock markets. While there are thousands of different stocks in the stock markets, there are only a few currency pairs in the forex market. Therefore, forex trading is less prone to price manipulation by big players than stock trading. Huge market volume also means that the currency pairs enjoy greater liquidity than stocks. A forex trader can enter and exit the market easily. Stocks comparatively is less liquid, a trader may find problem exiting the market especially during major bad news. This is worse especially for small-cap stocks. Also due to its huge liquidity of forex market, forex traders can enjoy better price spread as compared to stock traders.

Trading Hours & Its Disadvantage to Retail Stock Traders

Forex market opens 24-hour while US stock market opens daily from 930am EST to 4pm EST. This means that Forex traders can choose to trade any hours while stock traders are limited to 930am EST to 4pm EST. One significant disadvantage of retail stock traders is that the stock markets are only opened to market makers during pre-market hours (8:30am - 9:20am EST) and post-market hours (4:30pm - 6:30pm EST). And it is during these pre-market and post-markets hours that most companies release the earnings results that would have great impact on the stock prices. This means that the retails traders (many of us) could only watch the price rise or drop during these hours. Besides, stop order would not be honored during this time. The forex traders do not suffer this significant disadvantage. Also, a stock trader may supplement his/her trading with forex trading outside the stock trading hours.

Affordability

In order to trade stocks, a trader needs to have quite a significant amount of capital in his account, at least a few tens of thousands in general. However, a forex trader can start trading with an account of only a few hundred dollars. This is because forex trading allows for higher leverage. A forex trader could obtain larger transaction compared to stock market. Some forex brokers offer 100:1, 200:1 or 400:1. A leverage of 100:1 means that a US$1k in account could obtain a 100 times transaction value at US$100k. There is no interest charge for the leveraged money. Stock trading generally allows for not more than 2 times leverage in margin trading. There are interest charges associated with margin trading.

Data Transparency & Analysis Overload

There are thousands of different stocks in different industries. trader needs to research many stocks and picks the best few to trade. There are many factors that affect the stock prices. There are much more factors that may affects stock price than foreign currency exchange rates. The forex traders therefore can focus on few currency pairs to trade. On top of that, most data or news affecting currency exchange rate are announced officially, scheduled and in a transparent manner. Retail forex traders therefore have better chances of success than retail stock traders.

Bear/Bull Stock Market Conditions

Forex traders can trade in both way buying or selling currency pairs without any restrictions. However, stock traders have more constraints to trade and profit in bear market condition. There are more restrictions and costs associated with stock short selling. In a bull market when the economy is doing well, stock traders have a high chance of profitability if they buy stock first then sell it later. Savvy forex traders however, could operate in all market conditions.

Trending Nature of Currency

Major currencies are influenced by national financial policies and macro trends This national financial policies and macro trends tend to last long in a certain direction, either in monetary expansionary (rate cutting) or monetary contractionary cycle (rate hiking cycle). Stock prices however tend to fluctuate up and down due to many factors, many of these factors are micro and specific to the stocks. Therefore, forex traders can better exploit the trends in foreign currency markets that stock traders in stock markets.

Regulation

Generally, most major stock markets are better regulated than forex markets. Therefore, traders need to be aware of this difference to stock markets. Fortunately, there are however many reputable forex brokers in the market. With prudence and proper research, it is not difficult to find a suitable reliable forex broker.

Based on the above few points, forex trading seems to be a better trading option than stock trading, especially during these uncertainties in the global economy. During bull market condition, stock trading could be a viable alternative. A stock trader should definitely seriously consider supplementing their trading with forex trading. Forex trading enables a stock trader to exploit any opportunity arises during non-stock trading hours, by trading in forex trading. Forex trading would also enable the stock traders to understand a more complete big picture of world economies operations and further enhance their stock trading skills.

HOW TO CHOOSE A FOREX TRADING PLATFORM

It can be intimidating to choose a forex trading platform when you first start trading - here are some features that any good forex trading platform should have:

Security

Does the forex broker offer information about the security measures of its platform? Your trading and personal data should be encrypted, so that your money and identity are secure, whether you are paying and being paid through PayPal or online bank transfers.

The forex broker should also offer advice on how to increase your online security. Suspicion could arise of one that didn't because they might be making themselves liable if there are any problems.

Also, are there backup systems where your information can be stored in case of an IT problem?

Reliability

When can you use the forex trading platform? As forex is a 24hour a day market, 5.5 days a week, look for something that you can use constantly. Even when the market is closed, you want to be able to place orders to open when the market does.

The trading platform should also be efficient - if it is slow then the prices at which you are trading might be out of date. A good forex trading platform should update several times a second.

One-click trading

If a forex trading platform is unreliable, slow or prone to interruption, a trader can miss a quick opportunity. A platform that offers one-click trading will allow you to buy or sell forex contract with one click, which means there's no need to deal a ticket, and you won't miss the price you want.

Trading style suitability

Does the trading platform suit your trading style?

Is it easy to understand, or can it only be interpreted by a Wall street retiree? Look for a platform where it is easy to search for your market, and, if you want to trade more than forex, look for one that also allows you to trade on shares, options and indices.

Where are you trading from? If you use a Mac, can you use the platform on it? Likewise, can the program be accessed using different browsers and different smart-phone handsets?

Basically, does it do what you need? A good forex trading platform should be customizable to suit your trading strategy - does it allow automated trading, and does it allow you to micromanage every trade? The trading platform should be able to alert you to good trading opportunities, as well as accept complex orders, including the various stops and profits that the forex broker offers, so you can easily minimize your risk while maximizing your profits.

Charts

Does the forex trading platform have a separate charting platform, and how easy is it to navigate? And, if you want to trade from your iPhone or Blackberry, can you access these from your handset? And, can you trade directly from the charts, or do you need to deal a ticket?

Depending on your level of experience, you might want a charting package with a pattern recognition tool that will monitor the markets on your behalf, and could even let you know when the chart patterns are indicating trading opportunities.

And, if you want to trade forex throughout the day, it is essential that the charts are updated in real-time.

Market Analysis

Does your forex broker offer market analyses, and is this available using their trading platform or do you need to visit their website?

A good forex trading platform should include market analysis tools, including news feeds, in-house research and third-party research. As information is power, you want to be able to access as much of it as possible, and to have access to it without crawling the internet for the information you need.

Any trading that offers market analysis should also have historical data available, so you can see how the forex was affected when a similar situation occurred.

Price

Is the platform free? Many online forex trading platforms offered by reputable brokers are free, and your only costs will be if you make a loss.

If forex trading software isn't free, or if there is a nominal charge, find out what the added benefits are. And, if it isn't free, is there a money-back guarantee if you aren't happy with the software?

Also, does the trading platform offer the same pip spreads as the broker has advertised, or do you need to phone to get the best deal?

A pip is a 0.0001 unit of currency, and the pip spread is the difference between the buy and sell price of your currencies - so if the AUD/USD is quoted at 1.0578/1.0579, the sell price is

1.0578 and the buy price is 1.0579. For any spread, the price of the currency needs to make up the difference of the spread before you can make a profit. So, in the example, if you buy at
1.0579, the AUD only needs to rise two pips from 1.0578 to 1.0560 for you to make a profit. If there is a three pip spread, the currency would have to move by 4 pips before you made a profit.

Customer support

Is your forex broker just interested in getting you an account, or do they provide ongoing support for customers using the trading platform?

You should be able to email and/or phone your broker with questions ranging from placing trades to the button on your trading platform that isn't doing what you want.

Demo account

No matter how many questions you ask a customer support, it's hard to know how well a forex trading platform will suit you without being able to try it, so get online and see which companies have demo accounts available. The demo account should have all the functionality of the full account, or close to it.

HOW TO CHOOSE YOUR BROKER

More people are looking towards trading as a form of investment as well as a form of business. Forex Trading or Currency trading is fast becoming one of the most popular forms of investment trading today.

And with minimum startup capital required, the barriers to entry are fairly low and this has made it easier for the man in the street to start trading the Forex market.

However, unless you are a bank or large financial institution, you will require the services of a broker to be able to trade currencies.

Luckily, with an increase in the demand for FX Trading, there is a corresponding increase in the number of Forex brokers in the market.

However, with so many brokers to choose from, the problem facing most potential Forex traders is not how to trade but how to select a reliable broker to begin trading with.

Unfortunately, not all brokers in the market are the same. You will need to find a suitable broker that caters to your specific needs as a trader.

And from experience, this could be prove to be the tricky part as not all brokers offer the same services or have the same charges and policies. Slight differences in charges such as the pip spread will have a large impact on your profits' bottom line.

Seriously, if you wish to make a living as a Forex trader, you need to focus on the markets and not have to worry about questionable brokers. Therefore, choosing a reliable Forex currency trading broker should be one of the top priorities you need to do before you even start trading.

There are actually several factors that make a foreign exchange broker a good one, and here's my top 10 tips for choosing good currency trading brokers.

1. Reputation

Reputation is important in this business as there are quite a number of "fly-by-night" operations out there in the market. Basically, the rule of thumb is to stick with the more established Forex currency trading brokers who have a good track record.

An important factor to note is that all of their business dealings must be verifiable. Do they have a legitimate office with many satisfied customers? Have they been in business for many years or did they just pop up overnight?

You can find out a great deal of information from unbiased review websites that talk about their experiences with brokers. If someone got ripped off before, you should probably steer clear.

Dependable brokers should be transparent in their dealings and operations. Relevant information about how they function must be readily available online so that potential traders can easily find out more about their reputation as well as performance.

2. Regulations

No matter which country you live in, always choose a Forex broker that is conducting business in a country where their activities are monitored by a regulatory authority. A reliable Forex broker must be regulated and accountable to the relevant authorities.

For example, the Swiss banking system is one of the most tightly-run ships in the world regulated by the Swiss Federal Department of Finance, while US Forex trade brokers should be official members of the National Futures Association (NFA) and registered as a Futures Commission Merchant (FCM) with the Commodity Futures Trading Commission (CFTC).

In other words, they must adhere and conform to industry rules and regulations. The last thing you want is some unregulated broker in the middle of nowhere holding onto your money. If they go under, good luck ever getting your money back.

If a broker is not regulated by any monetary authority, it might be better to select another broker instead.

3. Differences in Pip Spread

Unlike stock brokers, currency trading brokers don't charge a fee or commission, instead they make their commission from the difference in the pip spread of the currency pair when you trade.

Unlike other financial markets, the currency market is not traded through a central exchange, the value of this spread is thus determined by the broker you are using instead.

Most Forex brokers publish live or delayed prices on their websites so that traders can compare spread differences and some brokers even offer a variable pip spread.

At first glance, the concept of a variable spread may appear tempting because of the volatility of the Forex Market. When the market is quiet, the spread is relatively small, but when the market really heats up, the spread difference might just widen large enough to wipe out your profits.

Unfortunately, many brokers out there are referred to as "bucket shops". They don't have your best interest in mind and some have been known to change the spreads around to their advantage.

The bottom line here is still to look for FX brokers with fixed and low pip spreads regardless of how the market moves.

4. Speed of Execution

In my book, this is something most novice traders seldom notice when they sign up for a trading account.

Most brokers do publish live prices on their trading platform but the question here is how fast are they able to execute the order once you click the "Buy" or "Sell" button.

Speed of execution of the order is imperative especially if you are a scalper trading the 5-minute charts, can't possibly sit around waiting another 5 minutes just for the order to confirm right?

Luckily, the best solution to this problem is to open a demo account with the broker and given them a test drive. This will allow you to test trial their trading platform's speed of execution.

5. Minimum Trading Account Size

Nowadays, broker leverages are getting higher and higher to cater for the small retail trader who have limited capital but wants a piece of the Forex action.

Micro and Nano accounts are available but most brokers offer the 2 standard types of trading account sizes, namely the Standard and Mini account.

There key difference between a Standard and Mini account is that a Standard account trades in 100,000 units, while a mini account trades only a tenth of that size, or 10,000 units per lot.

In other words the mini account deals in one tenth the size of the regular account. This allows you to risk a tenth of what you would be risking in the regular account.

6. Margin & Leverage

Margin accounts constitutes the basis framework of Forex trading, so make sure you are fully aware the broker's margin terms before rushing to open a live trading account, the last thing you want to hear is a margin call from your broker.

Make sure you are fully aware of how your broker calculates the margin requirements and does it change according to the currency pair traded? Is it fixed or variable at different times of the day or week?

Do take note that some brokers offer different margin requirements for Standard and Mini accounts, so beware.

And when it comes to leverage, most traders are familiar with the 1:100 ratio, but are did you know that some currency trading brokers today even offer leverages of up to 1:400.

A word of caution if you are a novice trader, don't use too much leverage as this is one of the key reasons so many newbie traders get wiped out so fast. Remember, the key to winning the Forex game is to compound small and consistent profits.

7. Rollover Rates

Rollover rates are charges that are incurred when traders move their positions to the following trading day.

If you are a scalper or a day trader, this rate might not affect your trading account but if you are a swing trader or a long term trader, this seemingly small figure might sometimes snowball if you are not aware.

That is why it is important to find out the minimum margin requirements to earn on an over-night position? Is it a mere 0.5% or a staggering 2%?

8. Trading Platform

A good trading platform should not only show real live prices that allows traders to "Buy" or "Sell", but also a host of other features like charting and technical analysis tools.

Some platforms even offer more advanced functions like trailing stops, mobile trading and even the use of automated trading softwares called expert advisers.

Most brokers will have their own proprietary trading platform but many are using the Metatrader 4 platform as it is a fairly easy to use system that can cater to all levels of traders ranging from novices to experts.

In my book, the type of trading platform used can either make trading the Forex market a breeze or a real hassle, so make sure you get a feel of the platform by signing up for a demo account. **9. Technical Support**

Typically, the type of support comes in the form of telephony or email support, and even "Live Chat" in some cases.

Since the Forex market is a global 24 hours market, likewise the corresponding support provided by the broker should be 24 hours around the clock as well.

Remember, it might be 3pm in the afternoon for you, but it could also be 3am in the morning for another trader across the globe, so ensure that there will be someone from the broker's office to pick up the call if something goes wrong.

An essential aspect of support that must be highlighted is the ability to close an "open" position over the telephone in the unfortunate event that your PC stalls or the internet connection fails, beware, anything can happen if Murphy's Law kicks in.

10. Additional Value-Added Services

Most of the better Forex trade brokers offer great value-added services in terms of free webinars, technical tools, e-books, articles and even daily market analysis and updates from their own panel of in-house consultants.

WHAT IS FUTURES TRADING

People who have no knowledge about futures contracts wonder, "What is futures trading?" Most of them think that it involves extraordinary financial risk and wealthy people. Though the two things often go hand in hand, this is not the case with futures trading. So, what is meant by trading futures? Futures are contracts to deliver a particular amount of commodity on a certain specified date in future. Some of the commodities which are normally traded include agricultural commodities like soybeans, wheat, rice or metals like copper, zinc, gold, or currencies.

Trading futures is entirely different from many other types of investing because a person who trade futures is not required to own or buy the commodity. A trader has to make his trading decision by speculating on the movement of price of a commodity in the near future. For example, if the trader believes that the price will move upwards, he will buy the commodity. Similarly, if he anticipates that the price will fall, he will sell the futures contract. If his prediction holds true, he will profit from the trade. On the other hand, if his speculation turns out to be wrong, he will incur loss.

A large portion of future contracts is traded by speculators; most of them liquidate their trading position before the expiry of the contract either making profits or incurring losses. In such a transaction, it is not the responsibility of the investor to deliver the commodity. Speculators play a vital role in the economy because they trade in bigger volumes which affect the price movements of commodities, and thus the economy. Hence, it is necessary to monitor trading volumes to get a clear picture of the price movements. Moreover, speculators make it easier for people who take actual delivery of the commodity to plan for the future. The real buyers and sellers feel comfortable knowing that there is always someone available in the market to buy the contract when the contract is being sold or sell the contract when the contract is being purchased.

However, trading futures is a long-term learning process. If you wish to trade futures, open an account with a reputed futures broker who has a good track record. Choose the commodity you wish to trade. And keep an eye on the market to determine price movements to determine your trading position. Use historical price charts, patterns, current news and other important indicators like moving average price and moving average convergence divergence (MACD), to ensure that your trading position is in accordance with these indicators.

Always check contract specifications to find out the trading hours of the contract, contract months as well as the last day of trading. You will gain experience when you actually trade futures. As always, there are high chances of incurring losses, if you are a beginner trader. Therefore, it is advisable to trade with a practice account first in order to gain sufficient knowledge and experience before real trading. The price movements and data available in practice account are real-time; hence, you will gain hands-on knowledge and experience without losing any money.

After getting acquainted with the futures market, start with a small investment; this will limit the amount of loss. Trade in a disciplined way and don't panic even if you lose in a particular trade. Analyze your strategy and make necessary changes, if any. After a period of time, you will be able to earn decent money, and you will never wonder, "What is futures trading?" like a beginner again.

Futures Trading in Currencies vs. Futures Trading in the Stock Market

In the stock market it is necessary to engage all trading through a broker or agent in matters of transactions and also receiving price quotes. Futures trading in Forex however have no middleman or agent so these costs are absent. This in turn increases investor's margins and decreases losses if incurred. These extra brokerage fees do skim away at investor profits and can add up to a significant amount for high volume traders.

Investors are advised to make portfolios to track past investments and track profits on various trades done. This serves as a tracker to allow investors to speculate on future investments.

Both futures generally work in the same manner. The key difference is that Forex futures are not traded in a centralized exchange, instead it is available in many different exchanges around the world. The majority of Forex futures are however done through the Chicago Mercantile Exchange and its partnering brokers.

Investors who wish to preview past market trends can visit Forex charts which aid in forecasting future results. Trend forecasting can never be 100% accurate and returns are not always guaranteed but this is common for any kind of trading.

This is why it is important for investors to continually monitor "predicting oscillators" in the charts to anticipate swings and fluctuations.

Despite there being no commission or transaction fees traders and investors will still lose a bit of their margin in the spread. The spread is the percentage difference in the buying and selling price of currencies. This is common in both regular Forex Trading and Forex futures trading. However, Forex futures trading is still considered the most lucrative form of trading according to research.

Both futures trading in stocks and currencies have their upsides and downfalls. Research and assessment show that futures trading in currencies are far less volatile then stock market trading. This, both reduces the chances for high profits or high losses. Risk-averse traders may find more comfort in Forex futures trading as a result of this. It is also shown to be more profitable in the long run compared to the stock market. It is also used by many to hedge currency fluctuations.

futures trading or commodity trading first started in Japan and in Holland, somewhere in 18th century. In US, commodity trading started by establishing a commodity market place in 1840s century. The market offered both sport delivery and futures contracts.

Futures trading differ from spot trading in different aspects. Spot trades are done for actual (and real-time) cash/product deliveries but futures are traded for hedging possible price uncertainties. Spot trades are done usually with a two-day cash delivery method where futures trades are done for usually 3 months durations. The futures trades for contracts which expire by next month or less is also often called spot trades.

The first products available for futures trading include meat, grains and live stocks. Later futures contracts for a variety of products were implemented including those for energy products, metals, currencies and currency indexes, stocks and stock indexes, and private and government interest rates. The CME (Chicago Mercantile Exchange) is responsible for the introduction financial features in 1970s, which very soon became the most traded futures type.

All futures have unchangeable contract specifications which are guaranteed by the clearing houses and margined to minimize counterparty credit risks. They are traded by open outcry of screen in public domain. Futures contracts are almost similar to forward contracts, and often the names are used interchangeably, but forward contracts are typically traded OTC (over-the-counter) through issuer-client or broker-dealer interactions where futures are traded through centralized markets.

Commodity futures are the most common form of futures and are traded all over the world. With the passing of time new and new agricultural, livestock and metal/natural commodities are becoming available for futures trading. Futures options are, like stock options, the right to buy or sell futures contract on a certain price at a specific time. A call futures option is the right to buy a futures contract and put futures option is the right to sell a futures contract.

Stock features or single-stock features are futures contracts for owning an underlying stock. Stock features usually have greater leverage and the holders of futures do not receive/pay any dividends. Stock index futures are meant for multiple purposes like hedging, trading and investing. Hedgers for owning stocks or index options, traders for benefiting from price volatility, and investors for achieving certain goals by not directly owning the stock. Currency features are futures contracts that enable the holder to buy or sell a currency at specified rate at a future date. As these futures are marked-tomarket daily, the forex investors can easily overcome the obligation to sell or buy currencies before the delivery date.

In US, the futures trading is regulated by CFTC (Commodity Futures Trading Commission). The major worldwide futures trading markets are CBOT (Chicago Board of Trade), CME, ICE Futures, Euronext.liffe, London Commodity Exchange, Intrade,

London Metal Exchange, TOCOM (Tokyo Commodity Exchange), NYMEX (New York Mercantile Exchange), NYBOT (New York Board of Trade), Sydney Futures Exchange, etc.

Futures Trading Brokers

Futures trading can turn out to be a profitable deal if proper research is conducted. It is therefore necessary to approach the right broker who considers the best interests of the trader, before actually going into futures trading. Research has shown that there are almost half a dozen firms operating. They offer an array of services ranging from full service, discount service, and online services Traders decide upon which futures trading company to approach, depending upon level of comfort with stock markets.

Even if the trader is aware of stock market, futures trading is entirely a different aspect, and it may require an amount of professional advice. A full-service broker ideally should have at least six years of experience in the industry. This broker can be an invaluable help for successful futures trading business. He can update his client about the economic trends, and effective methods of trading. They charge higher than most others but these costs are insignificant, in face of profits the broker can bring to business. The broker's knowledge and expertise can create wonders in trading.

Traders sometimes opt for discounted futures trading firms. It is done to reduce costs, in spite of getting the same services as the full-time brokers. It is advisable to keep trading with the old firm, until the reliability of the discounted trading firm is analyzed.

Online futures trading brokers are opted by veteran traders. They need continuous and instant connectivity to carry out different methods of trading. The commission rates for online firms are much lower. That does not ensure profitability, as it is necessary that a professional keep a watch on trade and advise right moves.

While selecting the futures trading firm the cost involved is not always important. Care is required in futures trading, and firm rich in experience protects the trader from risky investments that can ruin financial stability. There is no guarantee of this but efficient brokers can minimize and warn traders of possible pitfalls.

Benefits of Trading Futures

If we carefully look at the present business scenario then we could easily see that in recent time futures trading are gaining its world-wide popularity. In fact, it is the most common trading found on many markets these days. As per the latest definitions- it is more like a trading of contracts called futures contracts, which facilitates the owner with power to trade the basic commodity at somewhere in the future for a fixed rate. Moreover, like stocks and options trading, futures trades are done in precise centralized futures commodity trading markets. However, depending upon the type of futures contracts, it can be broadly classified as commodity futures contracts and financial futures contracts.

In commodity futures contracts, trading of contracts ends with a physical delivery. They may include agricultural commodity futures like sugar, oats, wheat, rice etc. or energy commodity futures such as crude oil, natural gas, etc.; metals & stones like gold, silver, diamond etc. This means that if a trader is holding a futures contract and the time come when it expires, the appropriate payment will be made by the buyer, and the basic commodity (agricultural or energy) will be delivered by the seller. Whereas in financial futures contracts, trading of contracts ends with a cash settlement and it include futures for treasury notes, bonds, mutual funds etc.

The futures contract trading can be executed electronically on electronic trading platforms linked to the major commodity exchanges or by the traditional open outcry method on the floor of the exchange. However, the basic form of futures contract is that it must state a location and date for physical delivery of the particular commodity. There are times when delivery arrangements are also specified by the exchange. This is particularly important for commodities that require high transportation costs, which in turn may affect the delivery place.

All those who are involved in commodity future trading must understand that for most commodity futures contracts, daily price movement limits are specified by the exchange. A limit movement is nothing but a move of price that can shift in either direction equal to the daily price limit. If the price moves down by an amount equal to the daily price limit, the contract is said to be limit down. And if the price moves up by the limit then it is said to be limit up. Price limits and positions limits generally aim to avoid large price movements deriving from excessive speculation. However, at times they act as an artificial barrier to trading when the price of the underlying commodity increases or decreases swiftly.

Overall, trading with commodity futures is definitely a good way to make handsome money but there are some essential factors that one has to take care. It is highly volatile in nature and more likely to remain unpredictable mainly because of several factors like geopolitical concerns, contracted demand supply fundamentals, growth and inflation pressures that put pressure on the global commodity market. It is a most interesting market environment but also a dangerous one as many wars have been fought and many nations & leading companies compete for scarce natural resources and food supplies.

Similarities between option and futures trading

Is options trading and futures trading really that different? What are some of the similarities? Well, there are actually four main areas in which options and futures are similar.

First of all, options and futures are both derivative instruments. This means that they are both merely contracts that allows you to trade their underlying asset at certain specific prices, hence deriving their value from price movements of their underlying asset. Both options and futures are merely contracts that bind the exchange of the underlying asset at a specific price. Without an underlying asset, options and futures would not have any value for their existence at all, which is why they are known as "Derivative Instruments". Options and futures both exist for the purpose of facilitating the trading of their underlying asset.

Secondly, both options and futures are leverage instruments. This means that both options trading and futures trading give you the ability to control the price movement on more of their underlying assets than your cash would usually allow. For instance, a futures contract with an initial margin requirement of 10% would allow you to control ten times the amount of its underlying asset than your cash would normally allow you to. A call option asking for $1.00 on a stock that is trading at $20 has a twenty times leverage as it allows you to control a stock worth $20 with only $1. Leverage also means that you could make more profit with options and futures on the same move on their underlying asset than you would if you bought the underlying asset with the same amount of cash. Of course, leverage cuts both ways. You could also potentially lose more than you would in options and futures trading than you would if you had simply bought the underlying asset.

Thirdly, both options and futures can be used for hedging. Hedging is one of the most important usages of derivatives. Both futures and options can be used to partially or totally hedge the directional price risk of an asset even though options are more versatile and precise as it allows for what is known as delta neutral hedging which allows a completely hedged position to still profit should the underlying asset stage a strong breakout in either direction. The hedging power of options and futures is also extremely important in reducing the downwards pressure faced by the overall market during market crisis because big funds and institutions can hedge the downside risk of their holdings using options and/or futures instead of selling their shares in order to maintain their account value. By reducing the amount of selling these big funds does, downside pressure in the overall market is partially relieved. Of course, this alone does not stop bear markets from forming when the general retail crowd (aka the "Herd") starts to rush out of the market.

Fourthly, both options and futures can be used to profit in ways other than the price movement of the underlying stock itself. Futures spreads can be used to speculate in seasonal price differences between the price of futures contracts of different expiration months and options spreads can be structured to profit from time decay no matter which way the underlying asset goes. Yes, it is these options strategies and futures strategies that make derivatives trading so interesting and so rewarding for people with the knack for mathematical calculations and strategies.

So, even though options and futures are very different derivative instruments and have very different rules and trading characteristics, they are still very much the same in the above areas and you can be a more comprehensive and savvier trader or investor by understanding how to use both options and futures to your advantage.

FUNDAMENAL AND TECHNICAL ANALYSIS

Fundamental analysis calculates future price movements by looking at a business's economic factors, known as fundamentals. It includes economic analysis, industry analysis and company analysis. This type of investing assumes that the short-term market is wrong, but that price will correct itself in the long run. Profits can be made by purchasing a mispriced security and then waiting for the market to recognize its mistake. It is used by buy and hold investors and value investors, among others.

Fundamental analysis looks at financial statements, including balance sheets, cash flow statements and, to determine a company's intrinsic value. If the price of stock falls below this intrinsic value, its purchase is considered a good investment. The most common model for valuing stock is the discounted cash flow model, which uses benefits received by the investor, along with the eventual price, the earnings of the company or the company's cash flows. It also considers the current amount of debt using the debt to equity ratio.

Technical analysis uses a security's past price movements to predict its future price movements. It focuses on the market prices themselves, rather than other factors that might influence them. It ignores the "value" of the stock and instead considers trends and patterns created by investors' emotional responses to price movements.

Technical analyses look only at charts, as it believes that all of a company's fundamentals are reflected in the stock price. It looks at models and trading rules based on price and volume transformations, such as the relative strength index, moving averages, regressions, inter-market and intra-market price correlations, stock market cycles and chart patterns. Chart patterns are the most commonly studied, as they show variation in price movement. Common chart patterns include "head and shoulders," which suggests that a security is about to move against the previous trend, "cup and handle," which suggests that an upward trend has paused but will continue, and "double tops and bottoms," which signal a trend reversal. Traders than calculate a security's moving average (the average price over a set amount of time) to clean up the data and identify current trends, including whether a security is moving in an uptrend or a downtrend. These averages are also used to identify support and resistance levels. For example, if a stock has been falling, it may reverse direction once it hits the support of a major moving average. Traders also calculate indicators as a secondary measure to look at money flow, trends and momentum. A leading indicator predicts price movements, while a lagging indicator is a confirmation tool calculated after price movements happen.

DIFFERNCES BETWEEN FUNDAMENTAL AND TECHNICAL TRADING

1. Purpose:

Fundamental Analysis: It seeks to forecast stock prices on the basis of economic, industry and company statistics. However, the most important variables considered in deciding stock prices are earnings and dividends.

Technical Analysis: It mainly focuses on internal market data.

2. Long-term & Short-term Price Movement:

Fundamental analysis: It seeks to predict long-term values of securities. Generally, the fundamentalist is a conservative who invests his funds for a long term. Long-term investors buy a high dividend paying stock and hold it for many years through market fluctuations.

Technical Analysis: The technical analysis determines the short-term price movements of the securities. The technician is a trader who buys and sells securities for short-term profits. He does not believe in buying and holding of securities. He gives importance to total returns, i.e., the realized price less the price paid, plus dividend received.

3. Value of Share

Fundamental Analysis: The fundamental analyst estimates the intrinsic value of shares and purchases them when their market price is less than the intrinsic value. He sells the shares when the market value of shares is more than the intrinsic value and earns profit. Thus, he works on long-term basis.

Technical Analysis*:* The technician believes that there is no real value to any stock. According to him, stock prices depend on demand and supply forces which in turn are governed by rational and irrational factors.

4. Finding the trend

Fundamental Analysis: In fundamental analysis, there is no scope for finding out the past trend of share and also the fluctuations in the price trend.

Technical Analysis*:* Technicians believe that past trend will be repeated again and the current movements can be used for studying the future trend. In other words, in respect of all securities there are cycles and trends which will occur again and again. Under technical analysis, charts and tools are used to compare various price movements. The technicians view price changes and their pattern mainly through price and volume statistics and tools such as Dow theory, Elliot Wave theory, pattern identification moving averages, advance or decline, charting styles, odd lots, short selling, put or call ratio, relative strength of indicators and Fibonacci levels.

5. Assumptions

Fundamental Analysis: There are no assumptions in fundamental analysis.

Technical Analysis: Technical analysis works on the basis of various assumptions which have been outlined earlier.

6. Decision Making

Fundamental analysis: The fundamental analysis carefully studies the financial statements, demand forecasts, quality of management, earnings and growth. Then they judge the prices of securities. Thus, the fundamental analysts are making decisions based on their own (subjective) opinions.

Technical Analysis: It listen to what the market has to say. So, the view of the market is the most important factor in determining stock prices.

7. Usefulness

Fundamental analysis: It helps identify undervalued or overvalued shares.

Technical analysis: It is useful in timing a buy or sell order.

TRADING PSYCHOLOGY

S.C.O.R.E. is acronym which stands for five traits or states which successful day traders implement in their trading. These traits/states are discussed in Jim Fannin's book *S.C.O.R.E. for Life,* which isn't a trading book, but the concepts have been adapted below to aid traders.

Self-Discipline

Of all the traits you need as a trader, self-discipline is one of the most important. It's required to implement a strategy effectively, and keep you from trading when your plan dictates you shouldn't.

Self-discipline is created and strengthened by excising self-discipline. There is no short-cut, and it isn't something you have or you don't. Anyone can create self-discipline through sticking to a plan. Each step of the trading process--from creating your trading plan, to executing it and monitoring performance--all require self-discipline because your mind will be constantly distracted by other things.

Say and write down how you will trade, then follow through. *Practice* self-discipline.

Concentration

Most day traders only trade one to four hours of the trading day--usually some combination of the first few hours and the last couple hours of the trading day. While a day trader's work day is shorter than most other professions, being focused and maintaining concentration is paramount. Each trade requires attention; one mistake can cost much more than a trader ever bargained for. Being slightly off on an entry or stop loss is the difference between a win and a loss; being a second too slow may mean missing a trade.

When an opportunity arises it must be seized, but opportunities aren't occurring all the time. A day trader must be able to focus on the market, without being drawn in when conditions aren't favorable, and still be able to act in a split second a trade trigger occurs.

Optimism

Believe in your approach. If you don't believe in your trading system--and that it will produce a profit over the course of days, weeks, months, years--it's almost impossible to trade the way you intend to. The more you believe in your plan, and are optimistic about its potential, the more likely you are to precisely implement it. If you aren't optimistic about it, why are you trading it? During the practice stage you attain a good idea of how your trading plan performs. After seeing repeatable success in your months of practice, your optimism should be at a point where you are confident in what you are doing, and *want* to follow your plan.

Relaxation

Concentration and optimism must be combined with relaxation. These three create an "in the zone" level of focus. When a trade signal is close at hand, your concentration is heightened. When conditions aren't favorable for trading you are more relaxed, giving your mind a break. Throughout the trading day you move from a state of focus to relaxation, and back again, over and over.

The relaxation is required. It doesn't necessarily mean putting your feet up, or distracting yourself with reading emails or watching TV. Instead, simply look away from the screen for a moment, take a few deep breaths, have a stretch or stand up for a few moments. You are aware of what is happening in your market, and watching for trades, but you're not on high alert. Trying to stay on high alert for the entire time you trade--even if it's only a couple hours--is exhausting, and may actually cause you to make more mistakes.

Take a few minutes every hour for relaxation.

Outside of trading, relaxation is important as well. Just as you shouldn't grind through even a few hours of trading without a breather, you shouldn't grind through days or weeks without taking some time for yourself. Relaxation recharges your batteries, making all your tasks more enjoyable...which in turn aids in performance. Don't neglect your health--psychical and mental. You stand the best chance of success if you are alert and capable of action when you need to be.

Enjoyment

Enjoy what you do. Seems simple enough, but many people begin trading for the wrong reasons.

Trade because you enjoy it; enjoy the challenge and the process of it. If you don't enjoy the challenge, then you won't succeed because the challenge will deter you.

Every successful trader I know loves the markets and trading. That enjoyment or passion is what drives them to create strategies, stick to them, and relentlessly implement their "edge" so they can continue to do this for a living.

S.C.O.R.E.

Self-discipline, concentration, optimism, relaxation and enjoyment are states all traders should try to emulate in their trading. They all work together to get you "in the zone;" a peak state where you are most likely to act (or not act) appropriately.

LEVERAGE

Leverage enables the traders to trade bigger amount of money by having a small amount of money in their accounts. Forex leverage has always been a controversial topic. The main question is whether it is more to help the traders, or it is mainly used as an advertising tool by Forex brokers to attract more customers, and then a good way to make the accounts become wiped out faster.

What Is Forex Leverage?

Forex leverage is just a broker side setting that enables the traders to take bigger positions with

a small amount of money in their accounts. It is the broker who can set your account leverage. You can't modify it on your own.

Let's say you have a USD live trading account with a broker. When the leverage is 1:1, then one dollar of your account works exactly as one dollar. Therefore, when EUR/USD rate is for example 1.2400, then you will have to pay $1.24 to buy one EUR against USD or to buy one EUR/USD.

When your account leverage is 1:2, it means each dollar of your account works as two dollars. Therefore, when EUR/USD rate is 1.2400, then to buy one EUR against USD, you have to pay $0.62:

$1.24 / 2 = $0.62

What if is your account leverage is 1:100?

Then each dollar of your account balance works as $100. Therefore, to buy one EUR against USD or one EUR/USD while the rate is 1.2400, you have to pay $0.0124:

$1.24 / 100 = $0.0124.

That is how Forex leverage works.

Is Forex Leverage a Facility for Traders or a Tool for Forex Brokers?

At the first glance, leverage looks like a nice feature and facility that brokers freely and handsomely offer to their clients. What is better than trading $1000 or $2000 by having $1 or $0.50 in your account? It looks like a nice feature that is offered for free.

I see that nowadays some Forex brokers offer even 1:1000 and 1:2000 leverage and accept the minimum deposit of as low as $100 to open an account.

There is no doubt that these brokers don't do this to help the poor Forex traders who cannot afford to open a big enough and reasonable live account. But the fact is 99.99% or I'd better to say 100% of those who open a $100 account with such a high leverage, will wipe out their accounts very easily. This is what brokers know better than anybody else.

Some of them even offer cash rewards if you open an account with them. For example, they add $50 to your account if you open a $100 account with them. The reason is that they do know that your $100 will be in their pocket, and the $50 they add to your account will never have to be paid to you, because you will never withdraw any money.

So, leverage is mainly a decoy to attract more retail traders who cannot afford to open big accounts. Professional Forex traders don't care about the leverage, because they calculate their position size carefully and precisely. They don't take more than a 2-3% risk per each trade setup. Therefore, leverage has no importance for them.

Forex Leverage Has Nothing to Do with Risk/Reward

It is recommended to take no more than a 2-3% risk per each trade setup. It means you have to choose the position size in a way that if it gets hit, you lose 2-3% of your capital. For example, when you have a $10,000 account and you have located a trade setup, you should choose the position size in a way that if you get stopped out, you lose $200 which is 2% of your account.

Unlike what most novice traders think, calculating of your position size has nothing to do with leverage. It depends on (1) the currency pairs and their pip value; (2) stop loss size; and, (3) the risk you want to take.

Also, leverage has nothing to do with pip value and the profit you will make. You can only make more profit by taking larger positions which is what a higher leverage helps you to do. But it can also cause you to lose more. That is why they say Forex leverage is a double-edged sword.

Leverage is related to the required margin. When your account has a greater leverage, you will need smaller required margin.

You can refer to the above example again. When your account leverage is 1:1, then you need a $1.24 required margin when you want to buy one EUR against USD while the EUR/USD rate is 1.2400. But when your account leverage is 1:100, then you will need $0.0124 required margin which is 100 times smaller.

Therefore, leverage enables you to take bigger positions with a smaller amount of money. But you can wipe out your account a lot faster and easier too. For example, when the price has to go against you for 100 pips to wipe out your account when your account leverage is 1:100, it can do it only by going against you for 20 pips to wipe out your account, when your account leverage is 1:500.

It means when a trader opens a $100 account with 1:500 leverage, then he will blow up the account sometimes with the first position he takes. It means Forex brokers don't care about you and your money. They care about making more money out of your losses:

Why Leverage Is Incorrectly Considered Risky

Leverage is commonly believed to be high risk because it supposedly magnifies the potential profit or loss that a trade can make (e.g. a trade that can be entered using $1,000 of trading capital, but has the potential to lose $10,000 of trading capital). This is based upon the theory that if a trader has $1,000 of trading capital, they should not be able to lose more than $1,000, and therefore should only be able to trade $1,000 (e.g. by buying one hundred shares of stock at $10 per share). Leverage would allow the same $1,000 of trading capital to trade perhaps $4,000 worth of stock (e.g. by buying four hundred shares of stock at $10 per share), which would all be at risk.

While this is theoretically correct, it is the way that an amateur trader looks at leverage, and is therefore the wrong way.

The Truth About Leverage

Leverage is actually a very efficient use of trading capital, and is valued by professional traders precisely because it allows them to trade larger positions (i.e. more contracts, or shares, etc.) with less trading capital. Leverage does not alter the potential profit or loss that a trade can make. Rather, it reduces the amount of trading capital that must be used, thereby releasing trading capital for other trades. For example, a trader that wanted to buy a thousand shares of stock at $20 per share would only require perhaps $5,000 of trading capital, thereby leaving the remaining $15,000 available for additional trades.

This is the way that a professional trader looks at leverage, and is therefore the correct way.

In addition to being an efficient use of trading capital, leverage can also significantly reduce the risk for certain types of trades. For example, a trader that wanted to invest in ten thousand shares of an individual stock at $10 per share would require $100,000 worth of cash, and all $100,000 would be at risk. However, a trader that wanted to invest in exactly the same stock with exactly the same potential profit or loss (i.e. a tick value of $100 per 0.01 change in price) using the warrants markets (highly leveraged markets), would only need a fraction of the $100,000 worth of cash (perhaps $5,000), and only the $5,000 would be at risk.

Trade Using Leverage

In other words, the more leverage the better. Professional traders will choose highly leveraged markets over no leveraged markets every time. Telling new traders to avoid trading using leverage is essentially telling them to trade like an amateur instead of a professional. Every time that I trade a stock, I always use the highest leverage I can (usually the options and warrants markets), and I would never trade a stock without using leverage (and the same goes for all of the professional traders that I know).

So, ignore all of the articles, comments, and even SEC warnings regarding leveraged trading, and the next time that you are making a stock trade, consider using a leveraged market instead.

INVESTING IN ECHANGE TRADED FUNDS

Exchange-Traded Funds (ETFs) are investment funds that aim to track the performance (value or price) of an index, a particular commodity or a group of commodities, or other financial products. For example, by buying shares of the DBS

Singapore STI ETF you are effectively investing in the 30 stocks (i.e., Singapore Telecommunications, Wilmar International, DBS Group, etc.) that are tracked by the STI (Straits Times Index).

Like other funds (Unit Trusts, Mutual Funds, etc.), ETFs invest in a portfolio of stocks, thus providing you, as the investor, access to a wide range of markets, sectors and asset classes. Unlike unit trusts, however, ETFs are listed on stock exchanges and are subject to brokerage commissions, just like shares on stock exchanges. (Unit trusts must be transacted through a fund manager, and are usually subject to management fees and/or sales charges.)

ETFs come in many different forms, including:

Bonds- Hold, or track the performance of, a basket of bonds (e.g. Singapore government bonds)

Equities- Hold, or track the performance of, a basket of stocks (e.g. stocks of Singapore companies; companies in emerging economies; global companies)

Commodities - Hold, or track the price of, a single commodity or basket of commodities (e.g. gold, silver, metals)

Currencies- Track a major currency (e.g. Euro)

In the US, there are ETFs that represent almost every sector of the market: stock indexes such as the Dow 30 or S&P 500; stock sectors such as healthcare, retail and technology; and commodity sectors such as agricultural products, gold or oil. There are ETFs for large companies, small companies, real estate investment trusts, international stocks, bonds and even gold and silver. Today there are also synthetic ETFs that use financial derivatives to mimic the performance of other ETFs, though these would not be suitable for the average investor because of the more sophisticated financial knowledge involved.

ETFs in Singapore

Here are some quick facts on ETF trading in Singapore:

• As of Feb 2011, Singapore had 75 ETFs with about S$3.2 Billion (S$3,200,000,000) in assets listed on SGX, the Singapore Exchange. By comparison, the Asia-Pacific region (excluding Japan) had about 190 ETFs with about S$52.5 Billion in assets by end-2010, while the US alone had about 1,100 ETFs with more than US$1

Trillion (S$1,270,000,000,000) in assets by Feb 2011.

• SGX has:

» Country ETFs for Singapore (3 ETFs), Australia (1), Brazil (1), China (6), India (5), Japan (3), Malaysia (2) and Russia (2), amongst others;

» Region-wide ETFs, including those for the Asia-Pacific (5), emerging markets (4) and global markets (2);

» Commodity ETFs for a broad basket of commodities (5) and gold (1);

» ETFs for Fixed-Income instruments (mostly bonds) and Money-Market instruments.

- As of Jan 2011, ETFs made up just 1.5% of trading volume on the SGX, compared to 14% in Europe and 40% in the US. However, growth has been dramatic: ETF volume on the SGX in 2010 was 45% higher than the volume in 2009.

- You can currently use your CPF savings to invest in 3 ETFs:

» ABF Singapore Bond Index Fund;

» streetTRACKS Straits Times Index Fund;

» SPDR Gold Shares Trust.

- ETFs can be transacted through your usual SGX listed stock brokers; the usual commission rate of between 0.18-0.28%, depending on amount, applies.

ETFs are best viewed as combining the risk diversification of unit trusts with the flexibility of stocks. They are a practical implementation of the philosophy of Index Investing which downplays picking individual stocks in favor of picking sectors, markets or geographical regions.

However, one should understand that, like any investment, ETF investments carry risks. Diversify even when investing in ETFs. It's advisable to spread your ETF investments amongst an ETF on precious metals, an ETF on the STI, an income ETF, an emerging market ETF, and an ETF on developed/global economies. This diversified portfolio is well within the means of the average Singaporean investor.

Finally, the fact that ETFs are listed on exchanges means that both investing strategies (e.g., a longer term, buy-and-hold approach) and trading strategies (e.g., a shorter-term, more active, buy-when-low and sell-when-high approach) become possible.

HOW YOU CAN BENEFIT FROM INVSTING IN ETF

An ETF is an Index Fund that is listed on a stock exchange and trades intraday (you can buy and sell it anytime of the day just like a stock). ETF can therefore describe as a Mutual Fund trading like a stock.

Although there are some very important differences between them, it's easy to understand ETFs if you think of them like mutual funds.

But unlike mutual funds, which try to beat indexes like the S&P 500 each year, ETFs try to follow them.

For example, if the S&P 500 trades 10 percent higher, the ETF that follows it will also trade 10 percent higher. If the S&P 500 index trades 12 percent lower, the ETF that follows it will also decline by 12 percent.

A Mutual Fund (also known as Unit Trust in Asia) is an investment vehicle that pools money from many individual investors. A professional fund manager then invests and manages these funds into a broad diversification of stocks, bonds and other securities.

The main problem with Mutual Fund or Unit Trust is that they tend to have high management fees and are very restricted in the way you can buy or sell them. With the explosion of ETF over the last few years, there is an increased skepticism with investing in Mutual Funds (Unit Trusts), except for some investment linked policies that are partly for protection purpose.

As ETF is relatively new as compared to Mutual Funds, that also means that there is currently few investors with the necessary skill and knowledge investing in it, thus providing a vast opportunity for early investors in this investment arena.

Imagine of those early investors who have invested and profited from the rise of China or the boom of Mutual funds in their early stage? You could be reaping a great return in your investment portfolio right now.

This will help put things in perspective: Back in the early 1970s, there were approximately 270 mutual funds in existence, with total assets of around $48 billion.

By 2006, the total number of mutual funds was approaching 7,000 ... with total invested assets of more than $9.2 TRILLION! **Who Issues ETFs?**

Do you want to find a comprehensive list of ETFs' currently in the market? A fairly comprehensive list is actually at Yahoo! Finance. If you go there, you'll find a section on ETFs under the "Investing" tab. It's not necessarily 100% current, but again, it's the best resource in the internet right now.

For the most detailed information on ETFs you'll want to go to the websites of the issuers of those ETFs. There you'll find a lot more information that will help you identify ETFs that you're comfortable buying.

Some of the major issuers include:

Barclays - iShares

State Street Global Investors - SPDRs (Spiders) and streetTRACKS

Merril Lynch - HOLDRSs

Rydex Financial - Rydex ETFs

Vanguard Group - Vanguard ETFs (formerly known as VIPERs)

ProFunds - Inverse and leveraged ProShares ETFs

Bank of New York - BLDRS (based on ADRs)

Some of the common ETFs:

Standard & Poors Depository Receipts, Series 1 (SPDR): (Ticker Symbol: SPY) A word about Ticker Symbols- Every stock ETF or Mutual Fund of Index has a ticker symbol assigned to it. For example, the ticker symbol for "Citigroup" is C and the ticker symbol for "S&P Depository Receipts (SPDR)" is SPY. Whenever you wish to trade a security, you have to type in the ticker symbol.

The SPDR (also known as SPIDER) is an ETF that tracks the performance of the S&P 500 Index. They are listed on the American Stock Exchange (AMX) and you can buy and sell them like the shares of any other company.

The DIAMONDS Trust, Series 1 aims to track the performance of the Dow Jones Industrial Index. They are listed on the American Stock Exchange (AMX) and it can be easily be bought or sold like the shares of any other company.

in Singapore, to grow your money at the same rate of the Straits Times Index, which measures the Singapore Stock market, then you can buy the STI ETF. You can buy a minimum of 100 shares through any local broker. The STI ETFs are priced approximately 1/1000th of the STI Index. So, if STI is at 2100, the STI ETF will be priced at $2.10/share. The wonderful thing about ETFS is that it also pays you cash Dividends of 3%-4% a year on top of the appreciation of the ETF's share value.

ADVANTAGES OF EXCHANGE TRADED FUNDS

ETFs offer the private investor a number of advantages. These include:

Market access:

As above, ETFs give investors unprecedented exposure to international stock markets, as they span nearly every available indexed equity class.

Cost:

ETFs are a cheap, efficient and direct means for investors to get exposure to equity markets. An ETF investment typically has low transaction costs (avoiding front-end charges, early redemption penalties or exit charges, and high service charges) and can be tax efficient.

Flexibility:

ETFs offer great flexibility for the individual investor, who is now no longer faced simply with the binary choice between direct stock ownership and diversification via mutual funds. The individual investor can trade in ETFs regularly, and can use ETFs in a variety of different ways. ETFs are publicly-traded products: since they are listed on exchanges, their prices are known throughout the trading day and they can be bought and sold the same way you buy and sell shares (online or via your broker), during local trading hours.

Tradability/Liquidity:

As above, ETFs have stock-like features, as they trade throughout the trading day at prices that generally reflect their net underlying asset value (provided that there is minimal tracking error).

Risk Diversification - ETFs allow you to achieve some degree of diversification: you gain access to multiple markets in a single transaction, with minimum investment and via a single platform.

Low Expenses- Total expenses for ETFs (0.3-1%) are usually lower than for unit trusts (1.5-3%); in fact, they are typically 0.65% in Singapore and even lower in the US.

DISADVANTAGES OF EXCHANGE TRADED FUNDS

While ETFs offer a number of advantages to the individual investor, it is important to also note their potential disadvantages. These include:

Novelty/Liquidity problems:

As noted above, ETFs are a relatively new financial product, especially for small investors, and this has raised some concerns about their true liquidity (although some commentators have dismissed the liquidity concern by pointing to the size of the markets in which ETFs are traded.) Furthermore, there appears to have been some misinformation circulated in the market place concerning ETFs. **The potential for tracking error:**

Some experts have claimed that the tracking error with ETFs (i.e. the difference between the price of ETF stocks and the true price of the asset/s they represent) can be substantial, leading to possible losses for the individual investor holding ETF shares.

Fund fees:

These may be substantial (depending on the fund).

Existence of Trading Costs - You must pay brokerage commissions to buy and sell ETFs, making ETFs more suitable for single, lump-sum investments than for small, regular investments. Investing in ETFs

TIPS FOR ETF INVESTORS

Any individual thinking of investing in an ETF and in ETF trading should ensure that they understand the following:

Market fundamentals and investment goals

As with other types of investment, individuals thinking of investing in ETFs should ensure that they understand the fundamentals of the market, and that they have articulated their own investment goals and concerns. They should understand what risks attach to investing in ETFs (e.g. potential counterparty risks), as no investment is risk free. They should also get to grips with understanding what the underlying assets are that the ETF is seeking to "mirror".

The different types of ETF

Investors should understand that there are now a variety of ETFs on the market, and should consider which one/s suit their needs best. Beginners in the market may be best opting for ETFs that mirror commonly understood stock indices.

The need for risk management

Investors should seek to manage their risks by ensuring that they are happy with each ETF's counterparties.

As with other forms of investment, investors should try to ensure that their ETF portfolios contain the right assets and that they are sufficiently diversified.

Novice investors may wish to avoid "leveraged ETFs", given their potential for generating losses.

The need to avoid over-complexity

Novice investors especially would be well advised to keep their ETF investments simple, especially in light of the increasing complexity of ETFs in the market place.

The need for cost minimization

ETF costs can be minimized by using an online broker (which should keep commissions to a minimum).

Investors should also ensure that their ETF portfolios are low fee and tax-efficient.

The need for advice

As always, should they have any doubts, investors should consult a market professional who is experienced in dealing with ETF investments.

RISKS INVOLVED IN EXCHANGE TRADED FUNDS

Tracking Error

ETFs are based on an index or benchmark. When there is a divergence in the return earned by the ETF from the index, you have a tracking error. In theory, tracking errors can be positive, meaning you will profit from the divergence or they can be negative, you receive less than the index would indicate. Usually, tracking error risk can reduce the performance of the ETF slightly.

Fees

The fees charged to run the ETF will negatively affect the return of the ETF relative to the index. While most ETFs have low expense ratios, be sure to add this item to your ETF risk assessment check list.

Index Matching

Managers of funds face several challenges including how to manage changes in the underlying index and what method to use to match the index. Some funds use a replication strategy, buying exactly the same stock at the exact same weights as the underlying index. Staying current with the index can raise trading costs, though it tends to reduce tracking errors after fees.

Other funds employ an optimization strategy, buying a subset of the underlying index's stocks, believing they will provide similar performance to the full portfolio as a lower trading cost. The extent the managers of the ETF use optimization techniques influences the size of the tracking error. The goal of optimization is to help reduce trading costs, which will lower fees.

Liquidity

With so many ETFs trading, there are a number of funds that are traded thinly, creating one of the more important ETF risks. Their bid ask spread can be quite wide. Whenever a security is not widely traded, investors may find it difficult to sell their ETF should they want to do so. Without ready buyers, you may find you have to lower your price further than expected to complete a sale. The same can take place when you are buying. Without a widely traded market, investors can find their orders go unfilled unless they adjust the price well beyond the current bid-ask.

Shares purchased on a highly volatile day-say, during a newsdriven 5 percent dip in an index on an otherwise flat trading day-can have a significant impact on long-term performance. This is especially true of an ETF that is not experiencing sufficient trading volume. Look for at least 100,000 average shares traded per day. More is better.

Narrowly Focused ETF

Narrow sector funds have a problem, because Securities and Exchange Commission (SEC) diversification requirements place restrictions on the construction of a portfolio. The basic ground rules for all mutual fund (including ETFs) are:

No single security can be more than 25 percent of the portfolio; and

Securities with more than a 5 percent share can't make up more than 50 percent of the fund.

For ETFs based on a narrowly focused index, these rules make it more difficult to match the underlying index.

Double Coverage

Creating a portfolio of ETFs might cause you to overweight a stock or sub-sector unintentionally. One of the advantages of an ETF is you are able to get exposure to a broader spectrum of the market or a specific sector. However, each ETF is comprised of individual securities that could change the original intention giving more exposure to a specific stock or sub-sector. Be sure to understand the underlying make-up of the index and the securities within the ETF to avoid encountering the risk of double coverage.

Knowing your ETF risk is part of your due diligence when evaluating an Exchange Traded Fund investment opportunity. While each of these risks might be considered a minor problem, they can add up to create sufficient risk to alter your final decision. Lower your ETF risk by knowing what you are buying.

A-Z TRADING DICTIONARY

A

ACTUALS
See Cash Commodities.

AGGREGATION
The policy under which all futures positions owned or controlled by one trader or a group of traders are combined to determine reportable positions and speculative limits.

AMERICAN STYLE OPTION
A call or put option contract that can be exercised at any time before the expiration of the contract. Most exchange listed options are American style options.

ARBITRAGE

The simultaneous purchase and sale of similar commodities in different markets to take advantage of a price discrepancy.

ARBITRATION

The process of settling disputes between parties by a person or persons chosen or agreed to by them. The National Futures Association's arbitration program provides a forum for resolving futures-related disputes between NFA Members or between Members and customers.

ASSIGNMENT

When an option is exercised by the holder of that option, the option is assigned to the writer of that option. The writer of a Call option is obligated to sell stock at the striking price of the Call option; the writer of a Put option is obligated to buy stock at the striking price of the Put option.

ASSOCIATED PERSON (AP)

An individual who solicits orders, customers or customer funds on behalf of a Futures Commission Merchant, an Introducing Broker, a Commodity Trading Advisor or a Commodity Pool Operator and who is registered with the Commodity Futures Trading Commission.

AT THE MONEY (ATM)

An option whose strike price is approximately the same as the current price of the underlying stock or future. For example, with IBM trading at $110, both the $110 call options and $110 put options are at the money.

B

BACKWARDATION

A futures market in which the relationship between two delivery months of the same commodity is abnormal. The opposite of Contango.

BAR CHART

A bar chart is a price chart that depicts each trading period month, week, day, hour, minute, etc.) as a vertical line ("bar") ranging from the low price to the high price. Most bar charts also include two small hash marks on either side of the bar: one on the left that denotes the opening price and one on the right that denotes the closing price.

BASIS

The difference between the current cash price of a commodity and the futures price of the same commodity.

BEAR CALL SPREAD

Net credit transaction. Maximum loss = difference between the strike less the credit. Maximum profit = credit. Requires margin.

BEAR MARKET (BEAR / BEARISH)

A market in which prices are declining. A market participant who believes prices will move lower is called a "bear". A news item is considered bearish if it is expected to result in lower prices.

BEAR PUT SPREAD

Net debit transaction. Maximum loss = debit. Maximum profit = difference between the strikes less the debit. No margin required.

BEAR SPREAD

A one-to-one spread established by selling a lower strike option series and buying a higher strike option series. Both option series are on the same underlying asset, are of the same type, and expire in the same month.

BID

The highest price anyone is willing to pay for a security.

BOARD OF TRADE

See Contract Market.

BLACK-SCHOLES

Fischer Black and Myron Scholes: the inventors of a formula to compute the values of European style call and put options.

BREAKOUT

A breakout occurs when price bursts out of a congestion pattern like a trading range, flag or pennant, or through some other support or resistance level. Sometimes "breakout" is used to describe upside moves only, while "breakdown" is used to describe downside breakouts.

BROKER

A company or individual that executes futures and options orders on behalf of financial and commercial institutions and/or the general public.

BUCKETING

Directly or indirectly taking the opposite side of a customer's order in the broker's own account or into an account in which the broker has an interest, without open and competitive execution of the order on an exchange.

BULL CALL SPREAD

Net debit transaction. Maximum loss = debit. Maximum profit = difference between strikes less the debit. No margin required.

BULL MARKET (BULL / BULLISH)

A market in which prices are rising. A market participant who believes prices will move higher is called a "bull". A news item is considered bullish if it is expected to result in higher prices.

BULL PUT SPREAD

Net credit transaction. Maximum profit = credit. Maximum loss = difference between the strikes less the credit. Required margin.

BULL SPREAD

A one-to-one spread established by buying a lower strike option series and selling a higher strike option series. Both options series are on the same underlying asset, are of the same type, and expire in the same month.

BUTTERFLY SPREAD

A long butterfly usually refers to the sale of two contracts on one option series and the purchase of one contract of a lower option series and one contract of a higher series. All contracts are on the same underlying asset, are of the same type, and expire in the same month. A long butterfly is also the result of combining a short straddle with a long strangle, or of combining a bull spread with a bear spread.

C

CALL OR CALL OPTION

An option which gives the buyer the right, but not the obligation, to purchase ("go long") the underlying contract at the strike price on or before the expiration date.

CANDLESTICK CHART

A price chart that uses rectangles that range from the opening price to the closing price of each trading session. The rectangle is dark (usually black) if the closing price is lower than the opening price (a down day), or light (usually white) if the close is higher than the open (an up day). Candlestick charts, which originated in Japan, are very similar to bar charts, although they pre-date them by a number of years.

The high and low price extremes extend as vertical lines above or below these rectangles, forming "wicks" to the bodies of the candles represented by the rectangles. Of course, if the high and low of the day are identical to the open and close, no wicks will exist; conversely, if the open and close are the same price, no rectangle (body) will exist. Like bar charts, candlestick charts can be constructed on any time frame.

CARRYING BROKER

A member of an exchange, usually a clearinghouse member, through which another firm, broker, or customer chooses to clear all or some trades.

CARRYING CHARGE

With regards to Futures, the cost of storing a physical commodity, such as grain or metals, over a period of time. The carrying charge includes insurance, storage and interest on the invested funds as well as other incidental costs. In interest rate futures markets, it refers to the differential between the yield on a cash instrument and the cost of the funds necessary to buy the instrument. *Also referred to as Cost of Carry.*

CASH COMMODITY

The actual physical commodity as distinguished from the futures contract based on the physical commodity. *Also referred to as Actuals.*

CASH MARKET

A place where people buy and sell the actual commodities (i.e. grain elevator, bank, etc.) See also Forward (Cash) Contract and Spot.

CASH SETTLEMENT

A method of settling certain futures or options contracts whereby the market participants settle in cash (rather than the delivery of the commodity).

CHARTING

The use of graphs and charts in the technical analysis of futures markets to plot price movements, volume, open interest or other statistical indicators of price movement. See also Technical Analysis.

CHURNING

Excessive trading that results in the broker deriving a profit from commissions while disregarding the best interests of the customers.

CIRCUIT BREAKER

A system of trading halts and price limits on equities and derivatives markets designed to provide a cooling-off period during large, intraday market declines.

CLEAR

The process by which a clearinghouse maintains records of all trades and settles margin flow on a daily mark-tomarket basis for its clearing members.

CLEARINGHOUSE

An agency or separate corporation of an exchange that is responsible for settling trading accounts, collecting and maintaining margin monies, regulating delivery and reporting trade data. The clearinghouse becomes the buyer to each seller (and the seller to each buyer) and assumes responsibility for protecting buyers and sellers from financial loss by assuring performance on each contract.

CLEARING MEMBER

A member of an exchange clearinghouse responsible for the financial commitments of its customers. All trades of a non-clearing member must be registered and eventually settled through a clearing member.

CLOSE (OR CLOSING PRICE)

The final trade price of the day (or other time period). In futures markets, the close is a representative price of the last minute of trading. In stocks, the close is the last recorded trade price.

CLOSING RANGE

A range of prices at which transactions took place during the close of the market.

CLOSING TRANSACTION

To sell a previously purchased option or to buy back a previously written option, effectively canceling out the position.

COLLATERAL

This is the legally required amount of cash of securities deposited with a brokerage to insure that an investor can meet all potential obligations. Collateral is required on investments with open-ended loss potential, such as writing naked Calls or Puts.

COMMISSION

This is the charge paid to a broker for transacting the purchase of the sale of stock, options, or any other security.

COMMISSION HOUSE

See Futures Commission Merchant.

COMMODITY EXCHANGE ACT (CEA)

The federal act that provides for federal regulation of futures trading

COMMODITY FUTURES TRADING COMMISSION (CFTC)

The federal regulatory agency established in 1974 that administers the Commodity Exchange Act. The CFTC monitors the futures and options on futures markets in the United States.

COMMODITY POOL

An enterprise in which funds contributed by a number of persons are combined for the purpose of trading futures or options contracts. The concept is similar to a mutual fund in the securities industry. *Also referred to as a Pool.*

COMMODITY POOL OPERATOR

An individual or organization which operates or solicits funds for a commodity pool. A CPO is generally required to be registered with the CFTC.

COMMODITY TRADING ADVISOR (CTA)

A person who, for compensation or profit, directly or indirectly advises others as to the advisability of buying or selling futures or commodity options. Providing advice includes exercising trading authority over a customer's account. A CTA is generally required to be registered with the CFTC.

CONDOR

A type of butterfly where instead of selling two options of the same series, two adjacent option series are sold.
See Butterfly Spread.

CONFIRMATION STATEMENT

A statement sent by a Commission Merchant to a customer when a position has been initiated. The statement shows the price and the number of contracts bought or sold. Sometimes combined with a Purchase and Sale Statement.

CONGESTION

Congestion refers to a period of non-trending or sideways price movement, often in a narrow range (or an increasingly narrow range, as in the case of triangles and pennants). See also Trading Range.

CONTANGO

A futures market in which prices in succeeding delivery months are progressively higher. *The opposite of* Backwardation.

CONTINUATION PATTERN

A continuation pattern is price action that interrupts a trend and implies a continuation of the trend (rather than a trend reversal) when the pattern is complete. Triangles, pennants, and flags are examples of continuation patterns.

CONTRACT MARKET

A board of trade designated by the CFTC to trade futures or options contracts on a particular commodity. Commonly used to mean any exchange on which futures are traded. *Also referred to as an Exchange.*

CONTRACT SIZE

The number of units of an underlying asset bought by exercising a call option or sold by exercising a put option. In the case of stock options the contract size is 100 shares of the underlying asset. In the case of options on futures contracts the contract size is one underlying futures contract. In the case of index options the contract size underlying asset is an amount of cash equal to parity times the multiplier. In the case of currency options it varies.

CONTRACT MONTH

The month in which delivery is to be made in accordance with the terms of the contract. *Also referred to as Delivery Month.*

CONVERGENCE

The tendency for prices of physical commodities and futures to approach one another, usually during the delivery month.

CORRECTION

A correction is a shorter-term countertrend move. See also Pullback.

COST OF CARRY

The interest cost of holding an asset for a period of time. This is either the cost of borrowing funds to finance the purchase, in which case it is called the real cost, or it is the loss of income because funds are diverted from one investment to another, in which case it is called the opportunity cost.

COVERED

A short option is considered covered if there is a corresponding offsetting position in the underlying security or another option where no margin requirement results from the short option.

CROSS-HEDGING

For example, hedging a cash commodity using a different but related futures contract when there is no futures contract for the cash commodity being hedged and the cash and futures market follow similar price trends (e.g. using soybean meal futures to hedge fish meal).

COX-ROSS-RUBENSTEIN

John Cox, Stephen Ross and Mark Rubenstein: the inventors of the binomial option pricing model.

CUP-AND-HANDLE PATTERN

A cup-and-handle is a reversal pattern formed when a market makes a rounded bottom (the "cup"), begins to rally, pulls back (the "handle"), and resumes the uptrend. See also Running Cup-and-Handle.

CUSTOMER SEGREGATED FUNDS

See Segregated Account.

D

DAILY RANGE

The daily range is the difference between the high price of the day and the low price of the day.

DAY ORDER

An order that, if not executed, expires automatically at the end of the trading session on the day it was entered.

DAY TRADER

A speculator who will normally initiate and offset a position within a single trading session.

DEFAULT

The failure to perform, for example, on a futures contract as required by exchange rules, such as a failure to meet a margin call or to make or take delivery.

DEFERRED DELIVERY MONTH

The distant delivery months in which trading is taking place, as distinguished from the nearby delivery month.

DELTA

This is the theoretical rate of change of an option's price relative to the price of its underlying, times the contract multiplier. Delta is positive for calls and negative for puts. An option with a delta of 25 will move 25% as much as the underlying asset. The delta of an option changes with the distance of the strike from the underlying. Delta also measures the equivalent unhedged position in the underlying asset.

DELIVERY

For example, the transfer of the cash commodity from the seller of a futures contract to the buyer of a futures contract. Each futures exchange has specific procedures for delivery of a cash commodity. Some futures contracts, such as stock index contracts, are cash settled.

DELIVERY MONTH

See Contract Month.

DERIVATIVE

A financial instrument, traded on or off an exchange, the price of which is directly dependent upon the value of one or more underlying securities, equity indices, debt instruments, commodities, other derivative instruments, or any agreed upon pricing index or arrangement. Derivatives involve the trading of rights or obligations based on the underlying product but do not directly transfer property. They are used to hedge risk or to exchange a floating rate of return for a fixed rate of return.

DESIGNATED SELF-REGULATORY ORGANIZATION (DSRO)

When a Futures Commission Merchant (FCM) is a member of more than one Self-Regulatory Organization (SRO), the SROs may decide among themselves which of them will be primarily responsible for enforcing minimum financial and sales practice requirements. The SRO will be appointed DSRO for that particular FCM. NFA is the

DSRO for all non-exchange member FCMs. See also SelfRegulatory Organization.

DISCLOSURE DOCUMENT

The statement that must be provided to prospective customers that describes trading strategy, fees, performance, etc.

DISCOUNT

With regards to Futures: (1) The amount a price would be reduced to purchase a commodity of lesser grade; (2) sometimes used to refer to the price differences between futures of different delivery months, as in the phrase "July is trading at a discount to May," indicating that the price of the July future is lower than that of May; (3) applied to cash grain prices that are below the futures price.

DISCRETIONARY ACCOUNT

An arrangement by which the owner of the account gives written power of attorney to someone else, usually the broker or advisor, to buy and sell without prior approval of the account owner. Also referred to as a Managed Account.

DIVERGENCE

A divergence occurs when two markets, or a market and a benchmark index, or a market and an indicator move in opposite directions. Common examples include one stock index (e.g., the Dow Industrials) moving higher while another stock index (e.g., the Dow Transports) moves lower, or when price makes a new high and a momentum oscillator (like the RSI or stochastics) makes a lower high.

The implication is that by moving in the opposite direction, the indicator (or secondary market or index) is not confirming the price move in the market from which it is diverging. Corrections or reversals sometimes result in such circumstances.

Note: Oscillators often produce multiple divergence signals in strongly trending markets before the trend actually reverses; view such signals conservatively.

DOUBLE BOTTOM

A double bottom is a reversal pattern consisting of two price troughs: The market declines to a new low, retraces, then falls again to the approximate price level of the first trough and retraces again. The implication is that by failing to break below the first price low, the market is hitting support and the down trend (especially if it has been an extended one) could reverse.

DOUBLE TOP

A double top is a reversal pattern consisting of two price peaks: The market rallies to a new high, retraces, then rallies again to the approximate price level of the first peak and retraces again. The implication is that by failing to penetrate the first price peak, the market is hitting resistance and the up trend (especially if it has been an extended one) could reverse.

DUAL TRADING

Dual trading occurs when (1) a floor broker executes customer orders and, on the same day, trades for his own account or an account in which he has an interest; or (2) a Futures Commission Merchant carries customer accounts and also trades, or permits its employees to trade, in accounts in which it has a proprietary interest, also on the same day.

E

EARNINGS PER SHARE

After-tax profits divided by the number of outstanding shares. This is one of the most important fundamental measures of a stock's prospects for future price gains.

ELECTRONIC ORDER

An order placed electronically (without the use of a broker) either via the Internet or an electronic trading system.

ELECTRONIC TRADING SYSTEMS

Systems that allow participating exchanges to list their products for trading after the close of the exchange's open outcry trading hours (i.e., Chicago Board of Trade's Project A, Chicago Mercantile Exchange's GLOBEX and New York Mercantile Exchange's ACCESS.)

EQUITY

For example, the value of a futures trading account if all open positions were offset at the current market price.

EUROPEAN STYLE OPTION

A call or put option that can only be exercised at the expiration of the contract.

EXCHANGE

See Contract Market.

EXCHANGE FOR PHYSICALS (EFP)

A transaction generally used by two hedgers who want to exchange futures for cash positions. *Also referred to as Against Actuals or Versus Cash.*

EXPANSION BREAKOUT/BREAKDOWN

A pattern from Jeff Cooper's book "Hit and Run Trading" that occurs when a new (two-month) high or low is made on a price bar with the largest daily range of the last nine days. See also "Breakout."

EXERCISE

This is the actual fulfillment of the terms of the options contract. The specified number of units of the underlying are bought or sold at the price predetermined in the option contract.

EXERCISE PRICE

See Strike Price.

EX-DIVIDEND

Means without dividends. Stocks purchased on the exdividend date are purchased without rights to the recent dividend. Owners of the stock are entitled to all future dividends.

EXERCISE
The demand of the owner of a call option that the contract size number of units of an underlying asset be delivered to him at the exercise price. The demand by the owner of a put option contract that the contract size number of units of an underlying asset be bought from him at the exercise price.

EXERCISE PRICE
The price at which the owner of a call option contract can buy an underlying asset. The price at which the owner of a put option contract can sell an underlying asset.

EXPIRATION
This is the date the option contract becomes void unless previously exercised. All stock and index option contracts expire on the Saturday following the third Friday of the expiration month.

EXTRINSIC VALUE
See Time Value.

F

FAIR VALUE

This is the mathematically calculated value of an option. It is determined by (1) the strike price of the option, (2) the current price of the underlying, (3) the amount of time left until expiration, (4) the volatility of the underlying, and (5) dividends.

FAR TERM

Expiration months further from expiration.

A mathematical series in which each consecutive number is the sum of the two preceding numbers: 1, 2, 3, 5, 8, 13, 21, 34, 55, 89, 144, etc.

FIBONACCI SERIES

As the series progresses, the ratio of a Fibonacci number divided by the immediately preceding number comes closer and closer to 1.618, the "golden mean," a ratio found in many natural phenomena as well as man-made objects like the Parthenon and the Great Pyramid. (The inverse, .618, has a similar significance.) Traders use various permutations of Fibonacci numbers to project retracement levels, among other things.

FILL OR KILL

Fill or kill (FOK). Trade orders that are canceled if they are not filled almost immediately (typically after being bid or offered three times), i.e., "If it doesn't get filled, it gets killed."

FIRST NOTICE DAY

The first day on which notice of intent to deliver a commodity in fulfillment of an expiring futures contract can be given to the clearinghouse by a seller and assigned by the clearinghouse to a buyer. Varies from contract to contract.

FLAG

A short-term congestion pattern (perhaps one to three weeks on a daily chart) that appears as a small consolidation within a trend. The upper and lower boundaries of the flag should be contained in horizontal trendlines; if the lines converge, forming a small triangle, the pattern is referred to as a "pennant."

FLOOR BROKER

An individual who executes orders on the trading floor of an exchange for any other person.

FLOOR TRADER

An individual who is a member of an exchange and trades for his own account on the floor of the exchange.

FOLLOW-UP ACTION

This is the term used to describe the trades an investor makes subsequent to implementing a strategy. Through these trades, the investor transforms one option strategy into a different one in response to price changes in the underlying.

FORWARD (CASH) CONTRACT

A contract which requires a seller to agree to deliver a specified cash commodity to a buyer sometime in the future. All terms of the contract are customized, in contrast to futures contracts whose terms are standardized. Forward contracts are not traded on exchanges.

FRONTRUNNING

A process whereby a futures or options position is taken based on non-public information about an impending transaction in the same or related futures or options contract.

FULLY DISCLOSED

An account carried by a Futures Commission Merchant in the name of an individual customer; the opposite of an Omnibus Account.

FUNDAMENTAL ANALYSIS

A method of anticipating future price movement using supply and demand information.

FUTURES COMMISSION MERCHANT (FCM)

An individual or organization which solicits or accepts orders to buy or sell futures contracts or commodity options and accepts money or other assets from customers in connection with such orders. An FCM must be registered with the CFTC.

FUTURES CONTRACT

A legally binding agreement to buy or sell a commodity or financial instrument at a later date. Futures contracts are standardized according to the quality, quantity and delivery time and location for each commodity. The only variable is price.

FUTURES INDUSTRY ASSOCIATION (FIA)

The national trade association for Futures Commission Merchants.

G

GAMMA

Gamma expresses how fast delta changes with a one point increase in the price of the underlying. Gamma is positive for all options. If an option has a delta of 45 and a gamma of 10, then the option's expected delta will be 55 if the underlying goes up one point. If we consider delta to be the velocity of an option, then gamma is the acceleration.

GAP

When the low of the current price bar is higher than the high of the preceding price bar, or the high of the current price bar is lower than the low of the preceding price bar.

Some traders also use the term gap to refer to an opening price that is higher than the high (or lower than the low) of the preceding price bar (an "opening" gap).

GENERALS

"Generals" refers to the major buy side institutions such as Mutual Funds.

GOOD-TILL-CANCELED (GTC) ORDER

A trade order that remains open until you cancel it (in practice, for perhaps 60 days; check with your broker); there is no need to re-enter it day after day.

GRANTOR

A person who sells an option and assumes the obligation to sell (in the case of a call) or buy (in the case of a put) the underlying futures contract at the exercise price. Also referred to as an Option Seller or Writer.

GUARANTEED INTRODUCING BROKER

A firm or individual that solicits and accepts commodity futures orders from customers but does not accept money, securities or property from the customer. A Guaranteed Introducing Broker has a written agreement with a Futures Commission Merchant that obligates the FCM to assume financial and disciplinary responsibility for the performance of the Guaranteed Introducing Broker in connection with futures and options customers. Therefore, unlike and Independent Introducing Broker, a Guaranteed Introducing Broker must introduce all accounts to its guarantor FCM but is not subject to minimum financial requirements. All Introducing Brokers must be registered with the CFTC.

GUTS

A strangle made up of in-the-money options with the underlying centered between the strikes.

H

HEAD-AND-SHOULDERS PATTERN

A reversal pattern consisting of three price peaks (in the case of a head-and-shoulders top) where the middle peak (the "head") is higher than the peaks on either side of it (the shoulders). A head-and-shoulders bottom is simply the inverse of this pattern.

HEDGING

The practice of offsetting the price risk inherent in any cash market position by taking an equal but opposite position in the (i.e. futures) market. A long hedge involves buying futures contracts to protect against possible increasing prices of commodities. A short hedge involves selling futures contracts to protect against possible declining prices of commodities.

HIGH

The highest price of the day for a particular contract.

HIGH-LEVEL PATTERN

A pattern that develops near the top of the recent trading range. For example, a consolidation that occurs at the top of an up trend could be called a "high-level consolidation." HISTORICAL VOLATILITY

The degree of movement in a market over a past time period, typically 100 days. It is normally expressed as an annualized percentage. A 100-day historical volatility of 32%, for instance, means that over the last 100 days the market has fluctuated in such a way that it would be expected to fluctuate about 32% in a year's time. If the market is currently priced at exactly 100, one would expect to see values between 68 (100-32% of 100) and 132 (100+ 32% of 100).

HOLDER

The purchaser of either a call or a put option. Option buyers receive the right, but not the obligation, to assume a position. The opposite of a Grantor. *Also referred to as the Option Buyer.*

I

IMPLIED VOLATILITY

The Implied Volatility of an option is a calculated value of the options pricing model. To calculate the implied volatility, an investor would use the last sale (bid price or asked price) as the theoretical value of the option and solve the model to determine what volatility would have been required to calculate that value.

IN THE MONEY (ITM)

An option whose strike price is below the current price of the underlying stock or future (for call options) or above the current price of the underlying stock or future (for put options). With IBM trading at $110, both the $100 call options and $120 put options are in the money.

INDEPENDENT INTRODUCING BROKER

A firm or individual that solicits and accepts commodity futures orders from customers but does not accept money, securities or property from the customer. Unlike a Guaranteed Introducing Broker, an Independent Introducing Broker is subject to minimum capital requirements and can introduce accounts to any registered Futures Commission Merchant.

INITIAL MARGIN

The amount a market participant must deposit into a margin account at the time an order is placed to buy or sell a contract.

INSIDE DAY

A day with a higher low and lower high than the preceding price bar.

INTRINSIC VALUE

The intrinsic value of an option is what its premium would be if the price of the underlying would remain at its current level until expiration. For an in-the-money option, it is the difference between it's striking price and the price of the underlying. The intrinsic value of an at-the-money or out-of-the-money option is zero dollars.

INTRODUCING BROKER (IB)

See Guaranteed Introducing Broker and Independent Introducing Broker.

J

No entries for J.

K

KEY REVERSAL

A one-day reversal pattern that occurs when a market makes a new high (or low), preferably a spike high (or low), and then reverses to close at or near the low (or high) of the price bar. The implication is that the market has experienced an extreme intraday sentiment change and a reversal is likely.

L

LAST TRADING DAY

The last day on which trading may occur in a given futures or option.

LEGGING

This is the term used to describe a risky method of implementing or closing out a Spread strategy one side ("leg") at a time. Instead of utilizing a "spread order" to insure that both the written and the purchased options are filled simultaneously, the investor gambles that a slightly better deal can be obtained on the price of the Spread by implementing it as two separate orders.

LEVERAGE

The ability to control large dollar amounts of a commodity with a comparatively small amount of capital.

LIMIT MOVE

The largest one-day price move allowed in a future contract, up or down. During limit up and limit down days, it is impossible for traders to trade at a price above a limit up move or at a price below a limit down move.

LIMIT ORDER

A trade order with a specified execution price, e.g., "Buy

100 shares of Microsoft at 147 3/4," or, "Sell 10 June Tbonds at 118 17/32 limit." Your broker cannot pay more than 147 3/4 for your shares or sell for less than 118 17/32 for your contracts.

A standard limit order is good for the remainder of the day it is entered unless you give specific instructions to cancel the order. At the end of the day, your broker will cancel the order automatically, and you will have to place it again the next day if necessary.

LIQUIDATE

For example, to take a second futures or options position opposite to the initial or opening position. TO sell (or purchase) futures contracts of the same delivery month purchased (or sold) during an earlier transaction or make (or take) delivery of the cash commodity represented by the futures market. *Also referred to as Offset.*

LIQUIDITY

The amount of trading activity, and thereby the ease with which you can get in and out of a market. Measured by volume (and open interest in the case of futures markets).

LOCAL

A member of an exchange who trades for his own account or fills orders for customers.

LONG

Purchasing an asset with the intention of selling it at some time in the future. An asset is purchased long given the expectation of an increase in its price.

LOW

The lowest price of the day for a particular contract.

LOW-LEVEL PATTERN

A pattern that develops near the bottom of the recent trading range. For example, a consolidation that occurs at the bottom of a downtrend could be called a "low-level consolidation."

M

MAINTENANCE MARGIN

A set minimum margin (per outstanding futures contract) that a customer must maintain his margin account to retain the futures position.

MANAGED ACCOUNT

See Discretionary Account.

MANAGED FUNDS ASSOCIATION (MFA)

The trade association for the managed funds industry.

MARGIN

See Collateral.

MARGIN CALL

A call from a clearinghouse to a clearing member, or from a broker or firm to a customer, to bring margin deposits up to a required minimum level.

MARK-TO-MARKET

To debit or credit on a daily basis a margin account based on the close of that day's trading session. In this way, buyers and sellers are protected against the possibility of contract default.

MARKET ORDER

A trade order executed immediately at the best possible price currently available, that is, "at the market." If you wanted to buy Microsoft using a market order, you could tell your broker, "Buy 100 shares of Microsoft at the market."

MARKET-ON-CLOSE (MOC)

Trade orders executed as market orders, but only during the closing of a particular market.

MARKET-ON-OPEN (MOO)

Trade orders executed as market orders, but only during the opening of a particular market.

MARKING A POSITION TO MARKET
The act of comparing the historic cost of a position to its current market value.

MAXIMUM PRICE FLUCTUATION
See Price Limit.

MCCLELLAN OSCILLATOR
The McClellan oscillator measures the momentum of market breadth by calculating the difference between the 40- and 20-day exponential moving averages of daily advancing issues minus declining issues on the New York Stock Exchange (NYSE).

The idea behind the indicator is that more stocks will advance than decline in bull markets and vice-versa in bear markets. Generally, markets are considered oversold when the oscillator is below -100, and overbought when it is above +100.

The McClellan oscillator is not a stand-alone indicator. It measures the trend strength of advancing and declining issues, and not necessarily market turns. Leadership in a handful of stocks has characterized many bull markets, defying the premise that the broad market must advance for stock indexes to hit new highs.

MEASURED MOVE

A price projection based on previous price swings. The idea is that different legs of a price move will be roughly the same length.

For example, if a stock trading at 100 rallies 20 points to 120, then pulls back 5 points to 115, a measured move projection would set a price objective of 135 if and when the rally resumes—another 20 point move from the low of the pullback.

MEDIATION

A voluntary process in which the parties to a futuresrelated dispute work with a neutral third party to find a mutually acceptable solution.

MINIMUM PRICE FLUCTUATION
See Tick.

MOMENTUM

As a general term, momentum refers to the speed or strength of price movement. It also is the name of a specific technical study that measure the difference between today's closing price and the closing price N days ago. See also Rate of Change.

MOVING AVERAGE

Moving averages are calculations that smooth price action to reveal the underlying trend. The following discussion uses daily closing prices to illustrate various moving average calculations. There are several types of moving averages. The most basic is the simple moving average (SMA), which is the sum of closing prices over a particular period divided by the number of days in that period.

For example, a five-day simple moving average would be the sum of the closing prices of the five most recent trading days, divided by five; a 20-day moving average would be the sum of the 20 most recent closing prices divided by 20, and so on. Each day the most recent closing price is added to the equation and the most distant day is dropped off.

A weighted moving average (WMA), the most simple of which is referred to as a linearly weighted moving average, multiplies closing prices by a weighting factor that emphasizes recent price action. The oldest price in the calculation is multiplied by 1, the second oldest by 2, the third oldest by 3, etc.

For example, a standard five-day weighted moving average would multiply the closing price of the fifth most recent trading day (five trading days ago) by one, the fourth most recent trading day by two, the third most recent trading day by three, the second most recent trading day by four, and the most recent trading day by five. These products would be summed and then divided by the sum of the weighting factors (in this case, 1 + 2 + 3 + 4 + 5 = 15) to derive the linearly weighted moving average value for the current day. Other weighting schemes can be used to increase or decrease the emphasis of more recent prices.

An exponential moving average (EMA) is actually a specific type of weighted moving average. It uses a constant (a smoothing factor) between 0 and 1 in the following manner: the current closing price (C) multiplied by the smoothing constant (S) added to the product of the previous day's exponential moving average value (PEMA) and 1 minus the smoothing factor, or:

Today's EMA = S*C + (1 − S)*PEMA

While the description and formula seems somewhat confusing, the approach is actually simpler to calculate than other moving averages because all you need is today's closing price and yesterday's EMA value.

Final notes: The preceding descriptions use daily closing prices. Moving averages can, of course, be constructed on intra-day, weekly or monthly time frames, and substituting the open, low, high or average price of a bar for the closing price.

One distinct type of moving average is the Adaptive Moving Average (AMA), which dynamically adjusts the number of days in the moving average calculation to current market volatility: In high volatility-periods the number of days would increase (making the average less sensitive and less prone to whipsaws), and in lowvolatility periods the number of days would decrease (making the average more sensitive to smaller price swings).

N

NAKED

A naked option strategy is an uncovered option strategy. It is an investment in which options sold short are NOT matched with either a long position in the underlying or a long position in another option of the same type which expires at the same time or later than the options sold. The loss potential with naked writing is virtually unlimited.

NAKED OPTION

See Uncovered Option.

NATIONAL FUTURES ASSOCIATION (NFA)

Authorized by Congress in 1974 and designated by the CFTC in 1982 as a "registered futures association", NFA is the industrywide self-regulatory organization of the futures industry.

NATIONAL INTRODUCING BROKERS ASSOCIATION (NIBA)

NIBA is a non-profit organization for guaranteed and independent introducing brokers.

NEAR TERM

Expiration month closest to expiration.

NEARBY DELIVERY MONTH

The futures contract month closest to expiration. *Also referred to as the Spot Month.*

NET ASSET VALUE

The value of each unit of participation in a commodity pool. Basically a calculation of assets minus liabilities plus or minus the value of open positions when marked to the market, divided by the total number of outstanding units.

NET PERFORMANCE

An increase or decrease in net asset value exclusive of additions, withdrawals and redemptions.

NOTICE DAY

Any day on which a clearinghouse issues notices of intent to deliver on futures contracts.

O

OFFER (ASKED)

The lowest price at which anyone is willing to sell a security.

OFFSET

See Liquidate.

OMNIBUS ACCOUNT

An account carried by one Futures Commission Merchant (FCM) with another FCM in which the transactions of two or more persons are combined and carried in the name of the originating FCM rather than of the individual customers; the opposite of Fully Disclosed.

ONE-EIGHTIES (180S)
A two-day reversal pattern for strongly trending stocks described by Jeff Cooper in his book Hit and Run Trading. For buys, on day one, the stock must close in the bottom 25% of its daily range. On day two, the stock must close in the top 25% of its range. The pattern is reversed for sells.

OPEN (OR OPENING PRICE)
The first trade price of the day (or other time period). In futures markets, the open is a representative price of the first minute of trading. In stocks, the open is the first recorded trade price.

OPEN OUTCRY
A method of public auction for making bids and offers in the trading pits of futures exchanges.

OPEN TRADE EQUITY
The unrealized gain or loss on open positions.

OPENING RANGE

The range of prices at which buy and sell transactions took place during the opening of the market.

OPENING TRANSACTION

The implementing of a new position.

OPEN INTEREST

The cumulative total of all option contracts of a particular series sold but not repurchased or exercised.

OPTION BUYER

See Holder.

OPTION CONTRACT

A contract which gives the buyer the right, but not the obligation, to buy or sell a contract at a specific price within a specified period of time. The seller of the option has the obligation to sell the contract or buy it from the option buyer at the exercise price if the option is exercised.

See also Call Option and Put Option.

OPTION PREMIUM

The price of an option.

OPTION SELLER

See Grantor.

OSCILLATOR

A technical indicator that measures (usually) the velocity of shorter-term price action to determine whether a market is overbought or oversold. Well-known oscillators include the relative strength index (RSI) and stochastics.

See also Momentum and Rate of Change.

OUT TRADE

A trade which cannot be cleared by a clearinghouse because the data submitted by the two clearing members involved in the trade differs in some respect. All out trades must be resolved before the the market opens on the next day.

OUT OF THE MONEY (OTM)

A call option whose strike price is higher than the market price of the underlying security, or a put option whose strike price is lower than the market price of the underlying security.

OUTSIDE DAY

A day with a high price higher than the previous day's high and a low price lower than the previous day's low.

OVER-THE-COUNTER MARKET (OTC)

A market where products such as stocks, foreign currencies and other cash items are bought and sold by telephone and other electronic means of communication rather than on a designated exchange.

OVERBOUGHT

When a market has presumably risen too far too fast and is due for at least a short-term correction. See Oscillator.

OVERSOLD

When a market has presumably fallen too far too fast and is due for at least a short-term correction. See Oscillator.

P

PAR

Par refers to a price of 100, e.g., "Stock XYZ rallied over par today, closing at 101 5/8."

PENNANT

A short-term congestion pattern (perhaps one to three weeks) that narrows into the form of a small triangle. (Pennants are essentially shorter duration triangle patterns.) See also Flag.

PIT

The area on the trading floor where trading is conducted by open outcry.

PIVOT

When a market is rallying and today's low is lower than the low of the highest day in the rally, that high becomes a pivot, or swing high. When a market is declining and today's high is higher than the high of the lowest day, then that low becomes a pivot, or swing low.

POINT AND FIGURE CHART

Point and figure chart. The point and figure chart differs from other price charts in that its time axis is not constant—prices are not plotted day by day or week by week, etc. Instead, point-and-figure charts use columns of ascending Xs and descending Os to portray up moves and down moves (of a certain magnitude), respectively, in a market.

For example, every X might represent a .5 point rise (referred to as the "box size") in the stock's price. Price declines would only be denoted by a column of Os if price fell, say, 1.5 points (three boxes, referred to as the "reversal amount"). In this case, if the stock rose from 25 to 25.5 to 26 to 26.5, you would add three Xs to your column of Xs, one for each .5 point rise from 25 to 26.5. If it rose only a quarter point or a half-point, or declined only a point, you would do nothing. Only when price dropped by 1.5 points or more would you stop adding ascending Xs and start a column of descending Os immediately to the right.

The larger the box size and reversal amount you use, the less sensitive your chart will be to smaller price fluctuations. Because a one-point move (or whatever increment you use for your box size) may occur in one hour or two days, the price action depicted in a point-andfigure chart is independent of time.

POSITION
This is the specific instance of a chosen "strategy". An option position is an investment comprised of one or more options.

POSITION LIMIT
The maximum number of speculative contracts one can hold as determined by theCFTC and/or the exchange where the contract is traded.

POSITION TRADER
A trader who either buys or sells contracts and holds them for an extended period of time, as distinguished from a day trader.

PREARRANGED TRADING

Trading between brokers in accordance with an expressed or implied agreement or understanding. Prearranged trading is a violation of the Commodity Exchange Act.

PRICE DISCOVERY

The process of determining the price of a commodity by trading conducted in open outcry at an exchange.

PRICE LIMIT

The maximum advance or decline, from the previous day's settlement price, permitted for a contract in one trading session. Also referred to as Maximum Price Fluctuation.

PREMIUM

This is the price of an option contract.

PULLBACK

A shorter-term countertrend move. Pullbacks offer opportunities to enter existing trends. See also Corrections.

PURCHASE AND SALE STATEMENT (P&S)

A statement sent by a Futures Commission Merchant to a customer when a futures or options position has been liquidated or offset. The statement shows the number of contracts bought or sold, the prices at which the contracts were bought or sold, the gross profit or loss, the commission charges and the net profit or loss on the transaction. Sometimes combined with a Confirmation Statement.

PUT

This option contract conveys the right to sell a standard quantity of a specified asset at a fixed price per unit (the striking price) for a limited length of time (until expiration).

PUT/CALL RATIO

This ratio, used by many as a leading indicator, is computed by dividing the 4-day average of total put volume by the 4-day average of total call volume.

PYRAMIDING

The use of unrealized profits on existing positions as margin to increase the size of the position, normally in successively smaller increments.

Q

QUOTATION

The actual price or the bid or the ask price of either cash commodities or futures or options contracts at a particular time.

R

RANGE

The difference between the high and low price of a commodity during a given trading session, week, month, year, etc.

RATE OF CHANGE

A momentum calculation that divides today's closing price by the closing price N days ago. Except for the scale, this study is virtually identical to the "momentum" technical study, which measures the *difference* between today's close and the close N days ago.

REGULATIONS (CFTC)

The regulations adopted and enforced by the CFTC in order to administer the Commodity Exchange Act.

REPARATIONS

The term is used in conjunction with the CFTC's customer claims procedure to recover civil damages.

REPORTABLE POSITIONS

The number of open contracts specified by the CFTC when a firm or individual must begin reporting total positions by delivery month to the authorized exchange and/or the CFTC.

RESISTANCE

A price level that acts as an overhead barrier to further price gains. Prices will frequently rally to these levels and then retreat. Resistance (like support) is rarely a specific price; it is more often a relatively contained price range, frequently in the vicinity of past technical patterns. One of the basic precepts of support and resistance is that once a support level is violated it becomes a likely new resistance level and when a resistance level is penetrated it becomes a new support level.

REVERSAL

A short underlying asset position protected by a synthetic long underlying asset position. The synthetic long underlying asset position consists of the combination of a long call option and a short put option. Both options have the same strike price and expire the same month.

REVERSAL PATTERNS

Price patterns that suggest a trend reversal rather than a continuation of the current trend. Double and triple tops/bottoms, head-and-shoulders patterns, cup-andhandle patterns, and V tops and bottoms are some examples of reversal patterns.

ROLLOVER

When one futures contract expires and the next contract in the cycle becomes the new front month.

ROUND TURN

A completed futures transaction involving both a purchase and a liquidating sale, or a sale followed by a covering purchase.

RULES (NFA)

The standards and requirements to which participants who are required to be Members of National Futures Association must subscribe and conform.

RUNAWAY

A strongly trending stock or future.

RUNNING CUP-AND-HANDLE PATTERN

A cup-and-handle pattern that occurs in an existing up trend. In this context, the pattern functions as a continuation pattern (a pause in the trend) rather than a reversal pattern. See Cup-And-Handle pattern.

S

SCALPER

A trader who trades for small, short-term profits during the course of a trading session, rarely carrying a position overnight.

SEGREGATED ACCOUNT

A special account used to hold and separate customers' assets from those of the broker or firm.

SELF-REGULATORY ORGANIZATION (SRO)

Self-regulatory organizations (i.e. the futures exchanges and National Futures Association) enforce minimum financial and sales practice requirements for their members.

SETTLEMENT PRICE

The last price paid for a contract on any trading day. Settlement prices are used to determine open trade equity, margin calls and invoice prices for deliveries.

SHORT

An obligation to purchase an asset at some time in the future. An asset is sold short given the expectation of a decline in its price.

SPECULATOR

A market participant who tries to profit from buying and selling futures and options contracts by anticipating future price movements. Speculators assume market price risk and add liquidity and capital to the futures markets.

SLIM JIM

A narrow-range, intraday consolidation pattern that forms at or near the high or low of the day. Generally, the longer and tighter the consolidation, the more explosive the eventual breakout.

SPIKE

A price bar that extends much higher or lower than the surrounding price bars.

SPOT

Usually refers to a cash market price for a physical commodity that is available for immediate delivery.

SPOT MONTH

See Nearby Delivery Month.

SPREAD ORDER

This is a type of order for the simultaneous purchase and sale of two options of the same type (calls or puts) on the same underlying. If placed with a "limit", the two positions must be traded for a specific price difference or better.

An oscillator based on the position of the current close relative to the absolute price range over the last N days.

STOCHASTICS

Stochastics consists of two lines: %K, which is the basic calculation, and %D, which is a moving average (typically three days) of the %K line. Usually, "stochastics" refers to an additionally smoothed version of the formula, whereby the original %D becomes the new %K line and a moving average of this line becomes the new %D line (this version is sometimes called "slow" stochastics, while the original calculation is called "fast" stochastics).

STOP ORDER

A trade order placed above or below the market's current price level that is intended either to liquidate a losing trade
(a "stop-loss" order) or to establish a new market position.

Stop orders become market orders as soon as their prices are touched. A stop-limit order specifies the worst price at which a stop can be filled, e.g., "sell 100 shares of DAL at
45 on a stop, 43 limit."

STRADDLE

A straddle is a long or short position in both call and put options. The options share the same exercise price, expiration month and the same underlying asset. A short straddle means that both call and put options are sold short. A long straddle means that both call and put options are bought long.

STRATEGY

An option strategy is one of various kinds of option investments, i.e. long call, covered write, bull spread, etc.

STRIKE PRICE

This is the fixed price per unit, specified in the option contract.

A price level that acts as a floor to further price declines. When a market repeatedly declines to a particular level and then rallies, the market is said to be "offering support" at that level.

SUPPORT

Support (like resistance) is rarely a precise price; it is more often a relatively contained price range, frequently in the vicinity of past technical patterns.

One of the basic precepts of support and resistance is that once a support level is violated it becomes a likely new resistance level and when a resistance level is penetrated it becomes a new support level.

SWAP

In general, the exchange of one asset or liability for a similar asset or liability for the purpose of lengthening or shortening maturities, or raising or lowering coupon rates, to maximize revenue or minimize financing costs.

T

TAIL

A new high bar that opens and closes near its low, or a new low bar that opens and closes near its high.

TECHNICAL ANALYSIS

An approach to analysis of futures markets which examines patterns of price change, rates of change, and changes in volume of trading, open interest and other statistical indicators. See also Charting.

THETA

This is the daily drop in dollar value of an option due to the affect of time alone. Theta is dollars lost per day per contract. Negative theta signifies long option positions or debit spreads; positive theta signifies short options or credit spreads.

THE "TURK"

A reference to what appears to be a calculated market stabilizing action by the Federal Reserve or its appointed ally, such as large broker-dealers who do program trading and are active in the futures. The Turk has had a tendency to "save the day" during many potential crisis occasions, such as when it looks like the market is about to crash.

TICK

A "tick" is the minimum price increment a stock, future, or option can trade in. For example, in a stock that trades in minimum increments of 1/16th of a point, a move of 1/16 up or down would be a one-tick move. In the S&P 500 futures, a tick is .10, in crude oil futures, a tick is .01, and so on.

TICK INDICATOR

The TICK indicator measures the difference between the number of up-ticking NYSE stocks vs. the number of down-ticking NYSE stocks throughout the day. (Do not confuse with the term "tick," used to describe a minimum price fluctuation.)

TIME SPREADS

A long time spread is created by selling a near term option and by buying a longer term option. Both options are on the same underlying asset, are of the same type, and have the same exercise price.

TIME VALUE

This is the amount that the premium of an option exceeds its intrinsic value. If an option is out-of-the-money then its entire premium consists of time value.

TRADING RANGE

Non-trending, sideways price action with fairly defined upper and lower boundaries.

TRAILING STOP

A stop order that is raised (in a rising market) or lowered (in a declining market) to follow an open position and lock in profits.

TRENDLINE

A straight line defining a price trend. Up trendlines connect the lows of several price bars while down trendlines connect the highs of price bars.

TRIANGLE

A longer-term (approximately a month or more on a daily chart) consolidation/continuation pattern in which prices progressively converge in a series of lower highs and higher lows.

TRIN

The TRIN indicator compares advancing issues/declining issues to the up volume/down volume ratio.

TRIPLE BOTTOM

A reversal pattern consisting of three price troughs at roughly the same price level. The implication is that by failing to move through such levels after three attempts, the market is meeting significant support and could reverse. See also "triple top," "double bottom," double top."

TRIPLE TOP

A reversal pattern consisting of three price peaks at roughly the same price level. The implication is that by failing to move through such levels after three attempts, the market is meeting significant resistance and could reverse. See also Double Top.

TRUE RANGE

A volatility calculation developed by Welles Wilder that modifies the standard range calculation by accounting for gaps between price bars. True Range is defined as the largest value (in absolute terms) of:

1. today's high and today's low (the standard daily range calculation);

2. today's high and yesterday's close;

3. today's low and yesterday's close.

Average True Range (ATR) is simply a moving average of true range calculated over N days. True range and average true range are common volatility measurements.

TWO-STEP PULLBACK

A combination of two pullbacks, where the second pullback tests the level of the first pullback. See Pullback.

U

UNCOVERED

See Naked.

UNDERLYING

This is the asset specified in an option contract, which, except in the case of cash-settled options, is transferred upon exercise of the option contract. With cash settled options, only cash changes hands, based on the current price of the underlying.

V

VARIABLE LIMIT

A price system that allows for larger than normal allowable price movements under certain conditions. In periods of extreme volatility, some exchanges permit trading at price levels that exceed regular daily price limits.

VARIATION MARGIN

Additional margin required to be deposited by a clearing member firm to the clearinghouse during periods of great market volatility or in the case of high-risk accounts.

VEGA

Vega is the sensitivity of an option's theoretical price to changes in volatility. It is the dollar amount of gain or loss, per contract, you should theoretically experience if volatility goes up one percentage point.

VOLATILITY

Volatility is a measure of the amount by which an asset has fluctuated, or is expected to fluctuate, in a given period of time. Assets with greater volatility exhibit wider price swings and their options are higher in price than less volatile assets.

VOLUME

The number of shares or contracts traded in a particular market in a given time period (usually day). See also Liquidity and Open Interest.

W

WAREHOUSE RECEIPT

A document guaranteeing the existence and availability of a given quantity and quality of a commodity in storage; commonly used as the instrument of transfer of ownership in both cash and futures transactions.

WEIGHTED MOVING AVERAGE

See Moving Average.

WHIPSAW

When price repeatedly thrashes above and below a moving average (or support or resistance level) triggering multiple false trading signals. The same term applies to indicators that behave similarly, e.g., when an oscillator like the relative strength index (RSI) repeatedly moves above and below its overbought or oversold level.

WIDE-RANGE DAY BAR

A high-volatility price bar, i.e., one whose range is much greater than the preceding price bars (or alternately, one with a range much greater than the average range over an N-day period).

WIRE HOUSE

See Futures Commission Merchant.

WRITE

An investor who sells an option contract not currently held (selling the option short) is said to have written the option.

WRITER

See Grantor.

X

No entries found.

Y

YIELD

A measure of the annual return on an investment.

YIELD CURVE

A chart in which yield level is plotted on the vertical axis, and the term to maturity of debt instruments of similar creditworthiness is plotted on the horizontal axis.

43813106R00094

Made in the USA
Lexington, KY
02 July 2019